ELECTING OUR PRESIDENT:
CAMPAIGNS AND ELECTIONS

by Jerry Aten

illustrated by Susie Kropa

cover by Jeff Van Kanegan

cover photo by Images and More

Publisher
Instructional Fair • TS Denison
Grand Rapids, Michigan 49544

ISBN: 1-56822-850-3
Electing Our President: Campaigns and Elections
Selected presidential portraits are reproductions from the
Dictionary of American Portraits published by Dover Publications, Inc., 1967
Copyright © 1999 by Ideal • Instructional Fair
a division of Tribune Education
2400 Turner Avenue NW
Grand Rapids, Michigan 49544

TABLE OF CONTENTS

★ ★

The President of the United States...
    As Defined Under the Constitution . . 1
The Electoral College 3
Winning a Presidential Election 5
Voting for Our President 9
Political Parties in America 11
The Road to the White House 14
The Primaries 16
The National Conventions 18
The Vice-Presidential Candidate 20
The Campaign 22
Press Coverage of the Campaign 24
Opinion Polls 26
Election Day 27

THE CAMPAIGNS AND ELECTIONS OF OUR PRESIDENTS

George Washington 29
John Adams 31
Thomas Jefferson 33
James Madison 35
James Monroe 37
John Quincy Adams 39
Andrew Jackson 41
Martin Van Buren 43
William Henry Harrison 45
John Tyler .47
James Polk 49
Zachary Taylor 51
Millard Fillmore 53
Franklin Pierce 55
James Buchanan 57
Abraham Lincoln 59
Andrew Johnson 61
Ulysses S. Grant 63
Rutherford B. Hayes 65
James A. Garfield 67
Chester A. Arthur 69
Grover Cleveland 71
Benjamin Harrison 73
Grover Cleveland 75

William McKinley 77
Theodore Roosevelt 79
William Howard Taft 81
Woodrow Wilson 83
Warren G. Harding 85
Calvin Coolidge 87
Herbert Hoover 89
Franklin Delano Roosevelt 91
Harry S Truman 95
Dwight D. Eisenhower 97
John F. Kennedy 99
Lyndon B. Johnson 101
Richard M. Nixon 103
Gerald R. Ford 105
Jimmy Carter 107
Ronald Reagan 109
George Bush 111
Bill Clinton 113

Election Trivia I 115
Election Trivia II 117
Election Trivia III 119

Answer Key 121

How to Use This Book

★ ★

The election process currently in use in the United States is a complex mix of history, modification, and even political maneuvering. This system is questioned with the approach of each presidential election. Many Americans would like to see presidents chosen by a direct election of the people. A number of efforts have been initiated to change to this method, but none has been successful.

Students will come to understand the historical reasoning that established the method of electing presidents under the original Constitution. They will also learn how and why the system has been changed. Each activity includes an information-packed reading followed by questions that require additional research, further analysis, or individual student opinion. The entire process comes alive with these short, yet meaningful, classroom assignments.

There is also a section of the book that focuses on the campaigns and elections that have elevated men into the most powerful position on earth—becoming president of the United States. From George Washington to Bill Clinton, students will learn about how they all got there. With short background profiles and explanations on the actual campaigns, students will come to understand how the system truly works through a discovery of the strategies and human drama that unfold during each campaign.

Also included are three trivia quizzes near the end of the book that can be used to test student comprehension of what has been presented or used merely as fun activities to be completed with the entire class. A complete answer key makes this a most comprehensive and valuable teacher resource to teach students about our election process.

THE PRESIDENT
OF THE UNITED STATES...
AS DEFINED UNDER THE CONSTITUTION

When the 55 delegates chosen to attend the Constitutional Convention met in Philadelphia in 1787, they were faced with a next-to-impossible task. They had to satisfy the various states involved and still create a framework that would establish a strong central government (a task the Articles of Confederation had failed to do). One of their main concerns was to create a hierarchy that would limit the power of any single individual. They certainly did not want to create a government that would allow for the possibility for another King George! Thus they wanted to create a system that would allow for a balance of power.

The result was the establishment of three separate and distinct divisions of government. Each would be responsible for making certain decisions, taking certain actions, and would be held accountable for those decisions and actions to the other two divisions of the government. Each branch would also have certain powers over the other two branches of government. The LEGISLATIVE branch of government would be responsible for making the laws. The JUDICIAL branch would be responsible for interpreting the laws and administering justice to those accused of breaking the laws. The EXECUTIVE branch would be responsible for enforcing and carrying out the laws of the land. The head of the executive branch is the president. He is called the CHIEF EXECUTIVE.

Under the Constitution, the president has these chief responsibilities.

- The president is commander in chief of the military and can send troops where he sees fit to protect the interests of Americans and the United States.

- As America's chief diplomat, the president meets with leaders of foreign nations and makes treaties with them subject to the approval of the U.S. Senate.

- The president is responsible for enforcing the laws made by Congress. He also has the power to approve or veto laws made by Congress.

1. The president of the United States is indeed a "man of many hats." In addition to the above responsibilities he has as defined by the Constitution, the president of the United States also wears these other hats. Find out what the president does when he fills the role for each of the following:

   Head of State _____

   Chief Foreign Policy Maker_____

   Chief Legislator _____

   Chief of Party _____

   Watchdog of the Economy _____

Article II, Section 4 lists the following qualifications for becoming president of the United States:

- Must be a natural-born citizen of the United States.
- Must be at least 35 years of age.
- Must have been a resident of the United States for at least 14 years.

2. What do you think of the age requirement for a U.S. president? Is it correct? Should the age be lowered to accommodate more potential candidates? Should it be raised to a higher age to ensure that the president is a person of experience? How old was the youngest person to ever become president? Who was this president? Who was the oldest man to become president?

   _____

   _____

   _____

The men who wrote the Constitution decided that the term of office for the president would be four years. They also determined that there would be no limit to the number of terms to which a president could be elected.

3. The Twenty-second Amendment to the Constitution changed this part of the original Constitution. Read the text of this amendment and explain below how it affected the original Constitution. Also explain why you think this amendment was deemed necessary.

   _____

   _____

   _____

THE ELECTORAL COLLEGE

When the delegates at the Constitutional Convention of 1787 came to the matter of how to elect their president, there was a great deal of discussion. It was obvious that the delegates did not want their president to function as their former King George had ruled Great Britain. They considered allowing the people to decide through a direct election. But a number of delegates feared that the citizens would not be well enough informed to make knowledgeable choices. Some of these delegates favored having the members of Congress choose the president. Then there were those who felt that the choice should rest in the hands of state legislators.

After much soul searching and a lot of heated debate, this compromise was reached. The president would be elected by electors that were chosen by each state. The state legislature would determine the manner in which the electors were to be chosen, but no member of Congress would be eligible to become an elector. It was felt that this would give the people themselves some voice in the matter, but that the electors chosen would be well informed about the candidates and the issues of the election.

Under the original system, the electors would meet in their state capitals and each elector would vote for two candidates. One of those candidates must live in a state other than that of the elector casting the vote. The ballots were then sent to the president of the U.S. Senate, who, in the presence of Congress, would open the ballots and count the votes. The person with the greatest number of votes would become president and the person with the second greatest number of votes would become vice president.

1. We all know that this part of the original Constitution has been changed. What was wrong with this original method for choosing the president and the vice president?

_____

_____

_____

2. How did the Twelfth Amendment to the Constitution change this method of electing our president and vice president?

_____

_____

_____

There was also a provision under Article II of the original Constitution which stated that if no candidate received a simple majority of the electoral votes cast, then the president would be chosen by the House of Representatives. In such an election, the top five candidates would be on a list given to the House, and each state would be entitled to one vote. Also, if there were a tie between two candidates, the House of Representatives would choose the president.

3. Research elections of the past and find out whether this has ever happened. Has the House of Representatives ever chosen the president? If so, when? Report your findings in the space below.

_____

_____

_____

4. How does the election you have described above give further evidence of the need for the Twelfth Amendment?

_____

_____

_____

There have also been changes in how the electors are chosen. Under the original plan, some states held direct popular elections to choose their electors. But in many states, the electors were chosen by the state legislatures.

5. Find out how this has changed by researching how electors are chosen today. Report your findings in the space below.

_____

_____

_____

_____

WINNING A PRESIDENTIAL ELECTION

When the men who wrote the Constitution came to the issue of how representation in the legislature would be determined, there arose a great controversy. Those who came from states with many people felt that the number of representatives should be based solely on population or head count. Those who came from the smaller states with fewer people felt that all states should have the same number of representatives in the body of lawmakers. The conflict over which of these two plans would be adopted threatened to break up the convention.

Finally, Roger Sherman of Connecticut stepped forth with a proposal he felt would satisfy both sides. He suggested that there be a two-house legislature. There would be an upper house called *the Senate*, in which each state would have equal representation. There would also be a lower house, the House of Representatives, in which each state would have one representative for every 30,000 inhabitants living in that state. This proposal satisfied both the smaller states, which feared domination by the larger states, and the more populous states, which felt they were getting equal representation with this plan.

When it came to the matter of electing the president, the same line of thinking followed. To satisfy both the populous states and those states with fewer people, the following plan was adopted: Each state would be entitled to the same number of electors as it had congressmen in the House of Representatives plus two (the number of U.S. senators in every state).

As the nation grew and more states were added, more electors were included in the electoral college. That number of electors was eventually frozen at 535. Then in 1961 the Twenty-Third Amendment to the Constitution granted the citizens of Washington, D.C., the privilege of voting for their president, too. It was determined that they should have three votes (the minimum number of electors a state can have), so the number of electors was raised to 538. At the beginning of each decade, a census is taken. Any major population shifts can result in states with large population gains getting additional electors, while those states that lose population may also lose electors.

Look in an almanac to find the number of electors each state had during the last presidential election and mark that number of electors within the boundaries of each state.

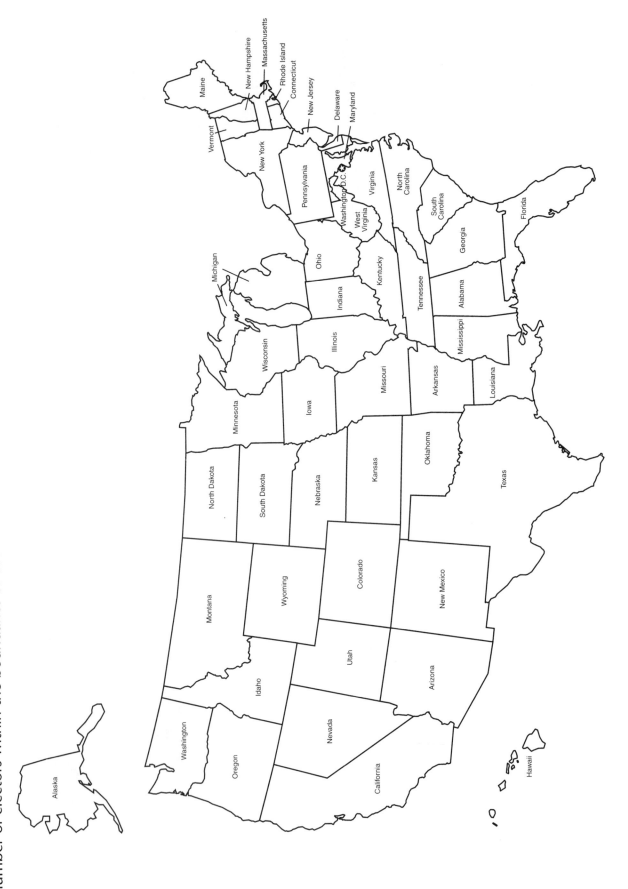

1. How many electors did your state have during the last election? _____

Throughout the history of presidential elections, the electoral college has often been criticized. There have been some changes since the original rules were established, but two huge criticisms remain. First, there is the criticism of the winner-takes-all rule. Under this rule, the people go to the polls on election day and cast their votes for their favorite slate of candidates (nominees for president and vice president). This is called the popular vote or the vote of the people. At day's end, when all the votes are counted, the candidate (and his running mate) who has the greatest number of votes from the people wins all of the electoral votes from that state! Thus a state with millions of voters could have a very close election in which one of the candidates wins by only a few votes, yet that candidate would receive all of the electoral votes from that state.

The other criticism is that there is no guarantee that an elector who is pledged to vote for a certain candidate will actually do so. Even though potential electors representing each major party are pledged to vote for their party candidate (should their candidate win the popular vote), there have been a number of examples in history in which an elector would stray from that promise when actually casting his/her electoral vote.

2. Look again at the map of electoral votes which you just completed. Which six states have the greatest number of electors?

    _____

    _____

    How many electoral votes are controlled by those six states? _____

3. Under the plan of the original Constitution, a candidate for president wins the election if he gets at least a simple majority of the electoral votes. A simple majority is defined as one more than half. Look at the number of electors currently available during a presidential election and decide how many electors are needed to win the presidency. _____

4. If you were running for president of the United States, where would you spend most of your time campaigning? Discuss your strategy below.

    _____

    _____

    _____

    _____

5. Which states have the smallest number of electoral votes possible?

    _____

    _____

6. Look in an almanac and cite at least ten presidential elections in which the winning candidate DID NOT WIN A POPULAR MAJORITY of the votes from the people. Note also the third-party candidates who helped to prevent the person who won the election from getting a majority of the popular vote.

_____

_____

_____

7. Who did your state vote for during the past presidential election? _____

8. Research the voting history of your state during presidential elections. Is there a trend that suggests historically that your state tends to vote for the same party during each election? Or is your state one of those that tends to move back and forth across the political aisle? Support your answer with factual data.

_____

_____

_____

9. Look once again at the map you completed of the number of electors to which each state is entitled. List the states and their number of electors in descending order until the electoral vote total reaches or exceeds the number necessary to win the presidency. How many states did it take?

_____

_____

_____

10. What is your own opinion of the electoral college? Is it fair? Or should it be abandoned in favor of allowing the vote of the people to determine the president? Use the back of this page to explain your opinion.

In early colonial days, very few people were allowed to vote. Only property owners who were white males over the age of 21 were afforded this privilege. When the framers of the Constitution met, they decided to leave this issue to the discretion of the individual states. Most states chose to continue the use of the above restrictions to define those who were eligible to vote. The Native Americans who were here long before the white man came could not vote. Neither could women. Even the few African Americans who did own property could not vote. Because of these restrictions and qualification requirements, fewer than 20 percent of the actual population were eligible to vote.

We all know that today men and women who are citizens of the United States and over the age of 18 are allowed to vote, regardless of their ethnic background, their religious affiliation, or their socio-economic status in life. But a number of Constitutional amendments were necessary before all this could happen.

Research the following Constitutional amendments and record below how each amendment affected the voting rights of Americans. Be certain to indicate the year in which each amendment was ratified and became law.

- Fourteenth Amendment

  _____

  _____

  _____

- Fifteenth Amendment

  _____

  _____

  _____

- Nineteenth Amendment

  _____
  _____
  _____

- Twenty-third Amendment

  _____
  _____
  _____

- Twenty-fourth Amendment

  _____
  _____
  _____

- Twenty-sixth Amendment

  _____
  _____
  _____

While the above Constitutional amendments vastly increased the number of eligible voters, there remain three restrictions on voting eligibility. Find out what they are and record them below.

1. Those who cannot vote in the United States:

   1. _____

   2. _____

   3. _____

2. If you were making the rules, would you change the voting requirements in any way, or would you leave them just the way they are? If you do think there should be any changes, what would they be?

   _____
   _____

3. Which presidential election will be the first in which you are eligible to vote? _____ Once you reach the age of 18, what must you do before you are allowed to vote? _____ When you become eligible, will you vote? _____

POLITICAL PARTIES IN AMERICA

When George Washington was elected unanimously by the electoral college as our nation's first president, there were no political parties in the young nation. However, during his administration, the party system began to emerge. There were those who wanted the federal government to be strong. Their concern came from seeing the failures of the Articles of Confederation, America's first plan for government, which had failed because the power had remained in the hands of the individual states. Those who believed in this political philosophy of vesting strength in the federal government became known as *Federalists*.

There were also those who believed that the power of the federal government should be limited. Their leader, Thomas Jefferson, advocated constant monitoring and evaluation of the powers given to the federal government. These people became known as *Democratic-Republicans*.

George Washington did not believe in political parties because he felt that they would divide the nation. But he did recognize their likelihood "in the course of time and things to come." By the time John Adams (who had been Washington's personal choice as his successor) sought the presidency, the two parties were firmly established, although there were no formal nominations. Adams represented the Federalists, and Jefferson was the candidate supported by the Democratic-Republicans.

As the nation began to develop, it became clear that political parties provided a good method for people with similar ideas on issues to band together to push for the success of those ideas. Many of those earlier parties have disappeared. The Democratic-Republicans eventually grew into the modern-day Democratic Party. By the election of 1856, the Republican Party had also become established, and the two major parties we know today had come into existence.

1. While the platforms of the two major parties may vary on different issues from one presidential election to the next, there are solid roots within each of these two major parties that remain stable with each election. Research the goals and beliefs of these two parties, then list at least three general statements you can make about the beliefs of the two major parties today.

Democrats

_____

_____

_____

Republicans

_____

_____

_____

2. Choose any election within the past two decades and research the voting results of that election. Look at the states won by each candidate. Then look at the results of the election just prior to or following the election you first researched. Were the results of the second election you chose similar to the first? Are there any conclusions you can draw about certain areas of the nation tending to vote in a similar pattern?

Election Year Chosen _____

Republican Candidate for President _____

Democratic Candidate for President _____

States Won by Republican Candidate _____

_____

States Won by Democratic Candidate _____

_____

Election Year Prior to or Following _____

Republican Candidate for President _____

Democratic Candidate for President _____

States Won by Republican Candidate _____

_____

States Won by Democratic Candidate _____

_____

Conclusions I Have Drawn:

_____

_____

_____

3. Trace the voting history of your own state through the past ten presidential elections. Which political party won the popular vote in your state? Was it the same in every election, or was your state one of those that did not vote the same way in every election? Record your results in the space below. Indicate the year of each election and the presidential candidate who won your state as well as his political affiliation.

_____

_____

_____

_____

4. Third-party candidates have also played important roles in the election process. Although no third-party candidate has ever won a presidential election, some have captured enough votes from one of the candidates to allow the other to win. Choose one of the following "third parties" and research the reason or reasons for which the party was born. Then summarize your findings in the space below. Choose only one of these:

Greenback Party; Free Soil Party; Bull Moose Party; Know-Nothing Party; Progressive Party; Prohibition Party

_____

_____

_____

_____

5. Choose one of the three strong third-party candidates, research the the reasons he chose to run, and indicate how strong a race he actually ran. Record your choice and findings on the back of this page.

Theodore Roosevelt in the election of 1912
George Wallace in the election of 1968
Ross Perot in the election of 1992

THE ROAD TO THE WHITE HOUSE

While our Constitution defines the requirements for being president as must be at least 35 years of age, must have lived in the United States at least 14 years, and must be a natural-born citizen, there are other unwritten qualifications that must be met even before a person can be considered seriously as a candidate for the presidency.

While George Washington had no reason to deal with the party system (because there were no parties when he was elected), any candidate aspiring to become president of the United States today must have a political affiliation. You learned in an earlier assignment about the political system and about how political parties play such a huge role in determining who becomes president. Any candidate seeking a party's nomination must believe strongly in what the party stands for and represents. The candidate will have a certain amount of influence on where the party stands on some of the issues but must believe in its general principles in order to have any chance at winning the nomination.

Having a strong track record in politics is also almost mandatory. In later assignments you will read the story behind each of our presidents and the road that person took to the White House. You will read about a few past presidents who had no political background whatsoever, yet they still won election to the presidency. However, in most cases it has been a case of starting at the local level, then proceeding on up to the level of state politics, and eventually earning a political name at the national level. Many of our former presidents were once members of the House of Representatives or the U.S. Senate. Some were governors of their home states, while other presidents won election after serving as vice president. The important point to remember is that in most cases the road to the White House is a long one that begins with years of building a political reputation.

1. Find out how many of our presidents were previously vice presidents. List all their names in the space below. (An almanac is a good resource to use for this assignment.)

_____

_____

_____

2. Another road to the White House taken by many presidents is a road already taken. A number of our presidents were incumbents when they were elected for another term of office. Most incumbents who have chosen to run for a second term have been difficult to beat. Find out how many incumbent presidents have been reelected for a second term and list their names in the space below. Beside the name of each incumbent, list the year in which he was elected to a second term.

_____

_____

_____

_____

3. While being an incumbent president has often resulted in reelection, there have been incumbents who did not win their bid for reelection. Find out the names of those who lost in their bid for reelection to the White House and list them below. Indicate the year of the election the president lost next to each president's name.

_____

_____

_____

_____

Once a potential candidate makes the decision to run for president, that candidate formally announces his availability at a scheduled news conference. The idea is to get immediate national exposure through the media. The timing is carefully planned and orchestrated by the candidate and his supporters. The announcement usually occurs in the early months of the election year. During each election year, there are a number of candidates whose names surface, then fade away as they discover they do not have the support necessary to win the nomination.

4. Choose a recent presidential election year and research the names of all those who announced their candidacy. Of course there will be the two major candidates, but your research should also include other candidates who "threw their hats into the ring" and announced their intention to run for president. Report your research on the back of this sheet.

THE PRIMARIES

Once a person decides to declare his availability as a candidate for president, the next step is to test his voting strength within the ranks of his own party. That is what primaries are all about. Under the original Constitution, there were no specific rules on how presidential candidates were to be nominated. In the early years the delegates who actually chose their party candidates were chosen by the party leaders who were recognized at the state level. Those party leaders in the big cities of the United States had a lot of influence. The common voter had virtually no voice in the selection of party candidates.

In 1903 the state of Wisconsin established a system in which ordinary, qualified voters could express their preference in a primary election that would allow them to vote for the delegates who would be sent to the party conventions. The idea was to allow them to vote within their own political party for delegates they felt would cast votes for the person they considered the best candidate. Shortly thereafter, primary elections became more direct by allowing voters to make a choice through a direct polling system. Today a majority of states use what is known as a closed primary, in which a voter must have previously declared himself or herself a member of a specific political party before he or she can vote in that party's primary election. When the primary election day arrives, the voter must sign in for the primary election of the party to which he/she has earlier registered.

There are also a few states that have open primaries, in which a voter may cross over and cast his or her vote in another party's primary election. In either case, a voter may vote in only one primary election. Some of the less populous states still express their candidate preference through the caucus system. This involves a series of meetings that begin at the local level, then proceed up to the county and eventually state level. During the state convention, those delegates chosen make the final decision on the candidate their party will support at the national convention.

In those states where presidential primaries are held, each state determines the month and the date when it will conduct its primary election. Some states hold their primaries shortly after the beginning of the year of the actual race. Their purpose is to allow candidates to test their strength early. Those candidates who do not fare well in these early primary elections usually drop out of the race soon. Those who show strength in these primary elections establish themselves as bonafide possibilities and are able to raise enough money from donations to continue their campaigns.

Iowa

#1 New Hampshire

1. Although it is not a very populous state, this state continues to hold the distinction of being the first state to conduct a presidential primary during each election year. Because of this, those candidates who are working toward the nomination flock to this state to spend both time and money to win the hearts of the voters. Find out what state ALWAYS holds the first presidential primary election.

   _____

2. How are primary elections different from the regular presidential election?

   _____
   _____

3. There are some objections to the primary system of choosing the nominees for president. One of these involves the physical strain that is placed on the candidates, who have to spend lots of time campaigning within the state in which the primary is being held. There is also the huge amount of money that is required of each candidate to become competitive through advertising. Research the philosophy of current primary elections and report any other objections people have to the staging of primary elections in the space below.

   _____
   _____
   _____

4. If the presidential primary system were to be abandoned, what type of system would you suggest to replace it?

   _____
   _____
   _____

5. Find out about your own state's ability to express its opinions concerning the candidates for president of the United States. Does it have a direct primary? Or does your state use some other method for allowing voters to be heard on the candidate of their choice?

   _____
   _____
   _____

THE NATIONAL CONVENTIONS

National political conventions are those huge, party-like meetings where the major political parties choose their candidates for the coming presidential election. Towering banners, posters, balloons, hats, campaign buttons, confetti, and band music are the essential ingredients during these upbeat meetings of the "best of the Democrats" and the "best of the Republicans." By the time the convention delegates actually cast their votes for their choice for the presidential nominee, the hoopla has reached a fever pitch that can only be described as overwhelming! The media is in force to snatch the slightest breath of drama and turn it into "media hype" for local, regional, or national newscasts.

This was not always the way it was done. Under the original Constitution, there were no set rules on how presidential candidates were to be nominated. Some of the earlier presidential candidates were nominated by congressional caucuses. As the political party system gained strength, there emerged a number of reasons for more structure and strategy in choosing candidates for the presidency.

1. The principal business of national conventions is of course choosing the candidates for president and vice president that will best represent the party. But there are other reasons for the popularity of the national party conventions that are so much a part of today's "Road to the White House." Read from other sources on national party conventions and report your findings on other reasons for such extravagant expense in the space below. (You should find at least two or three other reasons.)

_____

_____

_____

Throughout the history of national conventions, there has always been a certain amount of human drama. When there is more than one strong candidate involved in the race for the nomination, there is often bargaining among the delegates, and the secret formula is compromise.

2. When compromise does not lead to a consensus opinion among the delegates, party leaders sometimes choose a relatively unknown person as their candidate. Research this concept and record in the space below the name used to identify such unknown candidates.

_____

In today's world of politics, each state determines its own procedure for choosing delegates to the national convention.

3. To determine the number of delegates allowed to each state, a system is currently in use that gives each state a number of delegates equal to two times its combined number of U.S. senators and members of the House of Representatives. Under this system, how many delegates does your state have? _____

4. One of the purposes of national conventions is to come to agreement on a party platform. A party platform is the party's views on important domestic and foreign-policy issues. Consider yourself a candidate for president of the United States. What platform would you use to establish yourself as a desirable candidate within your party? List between three and five "position statements" that will identify and emphasize your values in today's world.

_____
_____
_____
_____

5. Where the parties choose to hold their national conventions is also important. Find out the cities chosen by each party during their most recent conventions and report their choices below. Also find out where the next conventions are scheduled to be held.

Under the original U.S. Constitution, there was a system for electing a president and a vice president that involved each elector being allowed to cast two votes. Electors were not allowed to cast both votes for the same candidate nor were they allowed to indicate which vote they wanted for president and which vote they intended for vice president. Each elector could cast one of his votes for a candidate from his own state if that was his desire; however, the other vote had to be cast for a candidate living in another state.

The logic behind this plan was an assumption that an elector would cast one of his votes for a resident of his own state and give the other vote to a political leader with a national reputation. Then, when all the votes were counted, a national figure would emerge as the winner and thus would become president. The Constitution also dictated that the person who received the second greatest number of votes would become vice president and also would be someone with a national reputation. But the emergence of political parties undermined this system almost from the beginning. Each political party began to put up two-man teams, and the electors chosen by that party would vote for both men. The election of 1800 became a classic example of the problems created by this early reasoning.

The Twelfth Amendment to the Constitution changed all this by providing that electors would vote separately for the offices of president and vice president. But the amendment generated another problem. Political parties often had wide areas of disagreement within their ranks, but they came together to unite as a party during election years. After the contest for the presidential nomination had been settled, the party leaders sought to console the losing faction by nominating one of its members for vice president. This came to be known as balancing the ticket. The problem with this plan was that if a president were to die in office, it would be highly probable that the vice president who would succeed him in office would hold entirely different views on many issues.

The issue has been somewhat resolved today by allowing the candidate who wins his party's nomination for president to consult with his advisors, then choose a running mate who maintains a position on issues similar to his own. This is all done in grandiose style and with great fanfare at the national convention following the party's nomination for president. There is still an attempt to balance the ticket, but this term has a different meaning today than it had many years ago.

1. The election of 1800 revealed some serious problems with the plan the men who wrote the Constitution created when they determined procedures for electing the president. Research this famous election and record below the events that revealed serious flaws in the logic of the framers of the Constitution.

   _____

   _____

   _____

   _____

2. Many of the early vice presidents were of the opinion that their role was of secondary importance and thus insignificant. They often felt this way because, under the original Constitution, the person with the most electoral votes became president and the person with the second greatest number of votes became vice president. In some cases the two were intense political adversaries. Often the president would not assign duties of major importance to his vice president. Under the original Constitution, what was the single responsibility of the vice president?

   _____

   _____

3. As the history of the country began to unfold, the role of the vice president began to change and gain greater significance, since the vice president succeeds as president if the president dies while in office. Research the history of elections and answer the following questions, which help to explain the emerging significance of the role of vice president.

   a. How many times has a vice president become president of the United States because the president died in office? _____

   b. Of those who did become president, how many were later elected president in their own right? _____ Who were they? _____

   _____

   c. Which vice president became president because the president resigned while still in office?

   _____

   d. How many full-term vice presidents were later elected president? Name them in the blanks below.

   _____   _____

   _____   _____

   _____

THE CAMPAIGN

In the early races for the presidency, candidates themselves did little to advance their chances to win by actively campaigning. Most candidates left the work of proving their worth to their campaign supporters. Advancing their own cause would have been considered too aggressive. With the election of 1824 came the first popular vote and with it a greater personal interest among candidates in how the public really felt about them. However, it was Abraham Lincoln who first stepped forth to advance his own cause by engaging in a series of debates with Stephen A. Douglas, his opponent for the United States Senate in 1858. Lincoln lost that election, but he gained a national reputation in the process. Two years later, when he ran for president against Douglas in the election of 1860, he realized the importance of actively campaigning on his own.

With the end of the Civil War and the completion of the transcontinental railroad, candidates were able to travel all over the nation spreading their message and charming the voters they hoped would come their way. Even though he lost the election of 1896 to William McKinley, Democratic candidate William Jennings Bryan used the railroad car to spread his message to everyone he could possibly reach. During a vigorous, three-month campaign, Bryan crisscrossed the nation, traveling nearly 20,000 miles, and addressing over 5 million people! Relying on only a few scant hours of sleep each night, Bryan spoke from the rear of his railroad car that made stops at literally every small town along the way. His strenuous campaign popularized the term "whistle stop campaign." From that point on, candidates began to see the value of personal campaigns.

Newspaper advertising was another medium through which a candidate could reach voters. Ads were relatively inexpensive and reached a large audience (anyone who subscribed or bought the newspaper), so they became quite popular as a way of appealing to voters.

By the mid-1920s candidates had begun to make use of the nation's airwaves by reaching the nation's voters via radio. And by the early 1950s, major presidential candidates began to travel by plane between major U.S. cities during their months of campaigning. The focus had shifted from the whistle-stops to the big cities, where many more voters could be reached. The big-city philosophy spread to a focus on the larger, more populous states. Those states that had the most electoral votes seemed to get the most attention from the presidential candidates. And why wouldn't they? Winning the electors of those populous states has become a giant step toward winning the presidency.

Television brought yet another dimension to the race for the White House as we know it today. The many commercials we see on TV during presidential campaigns may be less than appreciated by some of us, but they have become a vital part of the campaign strategy of today because of the number of people they reach. Millions of Americans are bombarded with a candidate's image and message every time one of those ads is aired.

Because of the impact of television advertising, parties developed a tendency to try to outspend each other in the hope of influencing voters. The logic behind this thinking is that the more times an image is presented to the viewer, the greater the chance of leaving a lasting impression. Consequently, parties and their candidates spend literally millions and millions of dollars on campaign advertising.

1. So where does all the money come from? Research the history behind the source of campaign funding and report your findings in the space below.

   _____

   _____

   _____

2. During the 1970s, laws were passed in an attempt to reform campaign funding. Find out what caused the rise in interest for campaign reform and record your thoughts below.

   _____

   _____

   _____

3. What new rules were enacted during the '70s to reform campaign financing?

   _____

   _____

   _____

Ever since Woodward and Bernstein (two investigative reporters from the *Washington Post*) uncovered the political scandal of Watergate during the early 1970s, reporting by the news media has taken on a much different twist. While some of us may think of it as more exciting, other people think it has created a much greater distrust in politicians.

In the early days political reporters stayed pretty much on course by reporting routine events as they happened without injecting their own "analytical opinions." There was a respect and concern for the private lives of politicians, and there was even good taste. For example, President Franklin D. Roosevelt's legs were paralyzed from polio. He wore leg braces and used a wheelchair. But reporters and photographers never revealed this disability to the public because they felt it would weaken his image as president.

After President Nixon resigned in the aftermath of the Watergate scandal, members of the news media began to be more skeptical and wary of politicians. It was almost as if they (as a group) began searching for almost anything they could dredge up that could be used to sully the reputation of a political leader. Many people feel that this brand of "negative reporting" has been at least partially responsible for Americans' declining trust in their political leaders. Opinion polls conducted over a period of years show that increasing numbers of Americans view politicians as dishonest and hypocritical. A recent poll revealed that nearly 80 percent of the public gave failing grades to elected officials on honesty and ethics.

Intense competition during the past 30 years has no doubt been the real culprit in this changing news media. The technology of today brings people news as it is happening—all over the globe! Cable television, satellite dishes, and the Internet have stepped up the pace of reporting the news. Fewer people are reading newspapers, so the competition for the consumer's attention further intensifies. News media reporting of political campaigns falls right in line with this growing trend. Critics say that reporters today have strayed from the real issues and the concerns of voters in favor of concentrating on the tactics and manipulations that are involved in the campaigns. They make the news features shorter, with graphics, pictures, and diagrams, and then they throw in their own "analysis," which more often than not contains negative comments.

1. An analysis of network news stories covering the 1996 political campaigns of George Bush and Bill Clinton found that there were three negative stories for every single positive news story about the candidates. Considering this kind of daily saturation, what kind of an image does this leave with voters about the candidates involved?

_____

_____

2. Journalists defend their coverage of the tactics and manipulations involved in campaigns as merely making citizens more sophisticated and better informed. What is your opinion of this comment? Are we indeed more qualified voters because we are exposed to the strategies and manipulations of the political parties and their candidates? Or does this only help to fuel our negative feelings about politicians and political parties?

_____

_____

_____

During recent years, critics of the media have called for significant changes in how political news is reported. They have asked for the following:

- more emphasis on the real problems of our nation and less on political conflict.
- more of what candidates are really saying and less "political analyzing" by reporters
- more on how politicians plan to improve America and less about their own personal lives

3. What are your own thoughts on these goals for media reform on political news? Are they good ones? Do you have others? Is reform really occurring in the media? Record your comments on the back of this sheet.

OPINION POLLS

The public has always been interested in poll watching as a way of monitoring the pulse of the voting public. While there were informal voting opinion polls taken as early as the 1820s, their informality led to their unreliability, hence their lack of credibility with the public. By the early 1900s, polls began to gain popularity among voters once again. It was George Gallup who helped to make the opinion poll one of the characteristic institutions of twentieth-century America. While he was director of research at a New York advertising agency, he founded the American Institute of Public Opinion. Gallup used the data he gathered in the form of market research to help clients on matters of government, business, and the news media. His methods became the standard because they were the most accurate and scientific to date.

Gallup attempted to choose a true cross section of America by asking voters from all segments of the population how they planned to vote. Soon other polls and political poll watchers sprang into action. But the presidential election of 1948 showed how "unscientific" those scientific methods could be. All three major polls predicted that Thomas Dewey would soundly defeat Harry S Truman. The Gallup Poll predicted Dewey by a margin of 49–44 percent, the Roper Poll indicated a 52–37 percent margin for Dewey, and the Crossley Poll predicted Dewey by a 50–45 percent margin. One Chicago newspaper even featured a front-page headline proclaiming "Dewey Defeats Truman." A very famous photograph shows a smiling Harry Truman holding the paper high because of the inaccuracy of the headline. In the late hours of counting votes, several states that were predicted to be won by Dewey were narrowly won by Truman.

Polls taken today are much more sophisticated than they were when Harry Truman upset Thomas Dewey over 50 years ago. In fact, the accuracy of polls today is really incredible. Read about the accuracy of today's political polls and report below reasons why the Dewey/Truman error would be virtually impossible today.

_____

_____

_____

ELECTION DAY

Presidential elections are held in November every four years. All years that are evenly divisible by four are years when presidential elections are held. The specific day for the election of our president was determined in Article II of the original Constitution. It stated that the election would be held on a date determined by Congress, but that the date should be the same in all states. While that date referred to the date when the electors would cast their ballots for the president, Election Day has been determined to be ". . . the Tuesday following the first Monday in November of all years evenly divisible by the number four."

As Americans, we consider the right to vote privately as one of our most cherished privileges. But voting privately was not always the way it was done. When individual citizens did finally gain the right to express their own feelings about who they wanted to be their president, they were forbidden from expressing their opinions privately. Instead, they were asked to call out their choice to an election clerk who recorded their preference. Voters often felt uncomfortable in this setting and were sometimes even intimidated by the election officials in charge. As time passed and the people began to voice their dissatisfaction with this system, Congress adopted the Australian ballot system as the blueprint to be used for voting in the United States. Under this system, voters were afforded the privilege of going into a voting booth alone. There are no hidden cameras nor are there any other people. It becomes strictly a case of the voter deciding within his/her own conscience entirely how he/she will express a preference.

When Election Day finally arrives, campaigning strategies are over! No one is allowed to pass out campaign literature or voice opinions designed to influence voters within a prescribed number of feet from the voting areas. Poll watchers carefully monitor this situation and report any violations that might occur. Polling places are in schools, churches, public meeting places, and even private businesses that are willing to provide space for this all-important day. Voting districts are known as precincts and are determined by where people live. Each voting place has election officials who are hired to check the validity of those who come to vote. They attest to whether the person is a legitimate, registered voter and lives within the voting district.

After properly signing the register, each voter is handed a ballot to take to the voting booth. The voter may be voting on a number of issues and offices. But heading the ballot of every presidential election are the voter's choices for president and vice president. Each party offers the voter a choice for a president/vice president team. Each voter can select only one of the teams as a preference.

1. Why do you think it is so important for voters to be allowed to express their voting preferences privately?

_____

_____

_____

2. The technology available today provides highly sophisticated voting analysis for use by the major television networks. In fact, they are in such competition to be "the first to declare a winner" that they often "declare a winner" even before the polls close on the West Coast. What kind of influence do you think this has on a voter in the Pacific Time Zone who has not yet voted? Would you be willing to spend the time and effort to go vote if you just came from a hard day of work and heard on your car radio as you headed toward the polls the name of the "declared winner"? How should this problem be solved?

_____

_____

_____

3. Research the number of electors available during a presidential election. How many are there?
_____ How many does it take to win? _____

4. When the voters express their choice for president during the popular vote, the next president is determined. However, it becomes official only when the members of the electoral college meet to cast their official ballots. When does this election take place?

_____

_____

GEORGE WASHINGTON

★ ★

Unlike the other U.S. presidents, George Washington's election to the presidency was not contested. There were no campaigns, because Washington had no competition. He so dominated the political landscape and was such an obvious choice when the first election was held in 1789 that not one of the 69 electors voted against him! What was there about this man that made him such a natural-born leader? To answer that question, we need to look at his background and early experiences.

Washington was born in 1732 near the mouth of Pope's Creek in Westmoreland County, Virginia. Little is known of his childhood other than that his father died when he was 11. Young George looked to his older half brother Lawrence, who was 14 years his senior, as something of a surrogate father. At the age of 16, he moved in with Lawrence at his estate called Mount Vernon. He looked forward to his twenty-first birthday, when he would inherit half of a 4,000-acre tract of land, three lots in Fredericksburg, and ten slaves as his portion of his father's personal property.

In school his best subject was math, and he later applied his mathematical mind to the occupation of surveying, which was much in demand in colonial Virginia at the time. He became the surveyor of Culpepper County, Virginia. When Lawrence died, Washington inherited Mount Vernon and turned it into a prosperous estate. He served in the Virginia militia for a number of years, rising to the rank of colonel. During the French and Indian War, he was recognized on a number of occasions for his expert military leadership.

In 1758 he resigned from the militia following his election to the Virginia House of Burgesses as one of the two representatives from Frederick County. During that time he led an expedition into the Ohio country to claim more than 20,000 acres for himself as a reward for his efforts in the French and Indian War plus tens of thousands more acres for the men who had served under him. He was a member of the Virginia delegation in both the First and Second Continental Congresses. Because of his past military experience, he was voted the overwhelming choice as the commander in chief of the Continental Army.

Inheriting a poorly trained army of undisciplined volunteers, he was able to accomplish a number of military victories by defeating superior forces with his cunning and sly tactics. His handling of men during the terrible winter of 1777-1778 was perhaps his most noteworthy military accomplishment. With inadequate food, clothing, and medical supplies, the army somehow survived. Perhaps even more remarkable was the fact that the troops spent much of the winter in training, and by spring those who survived had become crack military troops who were able to overwhelm the British and force the surrender at Yorktown.

When the Constitutional Convention met in 1787, Washington was unanimously elected president of the convention. When the Constitution was finally approved, he became the obvious choice as the young nation's first president.

ELECTION OF 1789

1. Washington's election as the nation's first president came in 1789. He was chosen unanimously by all 69 of the electors from the ten states. Find out which three of the original 13 states were not represented at this first election of a U.S. president and write their names in the space below.

   _____

   _____

2. George Washington was elected president unanimously in 1789 because he was the obvious choice as the finest leader, but also because there were no political parties as we know them today. Washington was a strong Federalist. Find out the political stand the Federalists took on the national government and explain their position in the space below.

   _____

   _____

ELECTION OF 1792

3. Washington was so universally supported that he was elected to a second term as president in 1792. Again he won the vote of every elector and carried all 15 states, winning all 132 of the electors. Who was Washington's vice president during both his terms of office? _____

4. In the election for president in 1789, Washington got the support of all 69 electors and was thus elected unanimously. His vice president received 34 electoral votes. In the election of 1792, Washington received all 132 electoral votes, again being elected unanimously. His vice president received 77 electoral votes. If Washington was elected unanimously, how do you explain the votes received by his vice president? (Hint: research Article II, Section 1 to explain your answer.)

   _____

   _____

5. While there were no political parties in 1789 and 1792 as we know them today, there were Federalists and there were Democratic-Republicans. What were the differences between these two political positions?

   _____

   _____

   _____

   _____

   _____

   _____

JOHN ADAMS

★★★★★★★★★★★★★★★★★★★★★★★★

Courtesy Independence National Historical Park

John Adams, our nation's second president, had a deep sense of compassion for humanity and genuinely loved people, but he never really learned to deal with human beings on an individual basis. He was born and grew up in Braintree, Massachusetts, the son of a farmer and leather craftsman. Adams' father was one of the true leaders of his community, being a selectman for Braintree Township. As a youth, John Adams preferred the pleasures of the outdoors to the boredom he felt while at school.

To please his father, who had always wanted him to go to Harvard, Adams enrolled there. He did graduate but finished slightly below the average rank in his class. Once he was admitted to the Massachusetts bar, Adams built a reasonably successful law practice in Boston. His political career began in 1770 with his election to the lower house of the Massachusetts legislature. In 1774 he was elected as a Massachusetts delegate to the Continental Congress, where he began to fuel the fires of rebellion against Great Britain. He also served on the committee that drafted the Declaration of Independence, although it was Thomas Jefferson who actually wrote the final document.

John Adams also served as a diplomat to France, but his discomfort with Benjamin Franklin caused him to resign his position within a year of his arrival. He served as America's first vice president during both of Washington's terms of office. He did not have a lot of love for the job and once said of his position: "My country has in its wisdom contrived the most insignificant office that ever the invention of man contrived or his imagination conceived."

ELECTION OF 1796
Adams was the logical choice of the Federalists, as he was wholeheartedly endorsed by the retiring President Washington. Thomas Pinkney of South Carolina was the Federalist candidate for vice president. His opponent was Thomas Jefferson, who headed a political group known as Jeffersonians. John Adams was characterized by the Jeffersonians as a despot who longed for an American monarchy. Jefferson, on the other hand, was viewed by the Federalists as a demagogue who preyed on the fears of the people to further his own political gain.

What the two men represented in reality were the strongly opposing viewpoints held by the two political factions. Adams did not trust the common people and believed in a strong central government, as his predecessor Washington had. Jefferson did not want the major power resting in the hands of a central government but felt that power should belong to the states themselves.

1. Based on this information, decide which candidate would support each of the following issues:

   a. _____ terms of U.S. senators should be for life

   b. _____ all powers of the federal government should be superior to any conflicting powers of the states

   c. _____ the powers of the federal government should be restricted and more powers reserved for the individual states to decide for themselves

   d. _____ distrusted Britain and still considered it our chief enemy even though the Revolutionary War was over.

   e. _____ would prefer to run the office of the presidency much as that of a friendly monarchy

   f. _____ supported the French Revolution and applauded the effort to overthrow the French royal family

2. Alexander Hamilton, although a Federalist, did not like Adams because he felt that Adams was too independent. So he devised a plan to deny the presidency to both Adams and Jefferson and deliver it to the Federalist vice-presidential candidate, Thomas Pinkney. Research this ploy and explain Hamilton's plan in the space below.

   _____
   _____
   _____

3. Why did Hamilton's plan fail?

   _____
   _____

4. In the electoral vote for the presidency in the election of 1796, Adams received 71 votes, Jefferson 68 votes. Thus Jefferson became Adams' vice president. Adams' presidency was marked by growing hostilities with France, and the insult of the infamous XYZ Affair brought America to the very brink of war with France. Research this famous historical incident and explain Adams' position on the matter in the space below.

   _____
   _____
   _____
   _____

THOMAS JEFFERSON

★ ★

Courtesy Bowdoin College Museum of Art

Thomas Jefferson, our nation's third president, was born on April 13, 1743, at Shadwell plantation in what is now Albemarle County, Virginia. Jefferson's father was a prominent landowner with title to over 5,000 acres of land in western Virginia. His early education taught him an appreciation of the classics. He studied law at the College of William and Mary under George Wythe before being admitted to the Virginia bar in 1767. Jefferson also developed an intense passion for writing while in college that would later be among his most distinguished accomplishments.

Few men who have run for the presidency have been as qualified as Thomas Jefferson. His long and impressive list of credentials includes the following: He was a member of the Virginia House of Burgesses. He was appointed to the committee charged with drafting the Declaration of Independence, and he became the logical choice to actually write the document because of his powerful use of prose. He was a member of the Virginia House of Delegates and was elected governor of Virginia. Jefferson was a member of the Continental Congress in the early 1780s and served as our minister to France from 1785 to 1789. Under President George Washington, he was the nation's first secretary of state. Finally, he received the second greatest number of electoral votes in the presidential election of 1796. Thus he served as vice president in the John Adams administration, a position he considered insignificant and somewhat belittling.

ELECTION OF 1800

Jefferson was clearly the leader and the choice of the Republican party, which was growing in popularity in the young nation. Aaron Burr was the party's choice for vice president. President John Adams was the Federalist choice for president and Charles Cotesworth Pinckney was their vice-presidential candidate.

Jefferson considered religion a personal matter and favored a strict separation of church and state. However, his political opponents, who favored state-supported religion, urged voters to choose "God . . . and a religious president" over "Jefferson . . . and no God." Federalist supporters denounced him as an atheist. Perhaps the most important issue in this election was the matter of federal authority versus states' rights. Jefferson and James Madison had written the controversial Virginia and Kentucky Resolutions, which declared the Alien and Sedition Acts unconstitutional. The principle of state nullification of federal laws did not prevail, but the resolutions became a rallying point for the anti-Federalists and the Republicans. With Adams losing the electors of New York, his defeat became inevitable. With the Republicans in charge, it seemed obvious that Jefferson would win the election.

1. Because each elector was allowed to vote for two candidates, both Jefferson and Aaron Burr received 73 electoral votes. President John Adams received 65 votes. Even though it had always been clear during the campaign that Jefferson was the presidential candidate and Burr the vice-presidential candidate, Burr refused to concede. Thus the election was sent to the House of Representatives. Research this historical incident and report the outcome in the space below.

   _____

   _____

   _____

2. The results of the election of 1800 prompted the passage of the Twelfth Amendment to the Constitution. Look closely at the Twelfth Amendment and describe below how it changed the manner in which presidents were elected.

   _____

   _____

   _____

ELECTION OF 1804

Because of his success as president, Thomas Jefferson was the unanimous choice as the Republican candidate for president in 1804. George Clinton of New York was nominated for vice president. The opposing Federalist party chose Charles Cotesworth Pinckney as its candidate with Rufus King as its candidate for vice president.

The Federalist Party was a party in decline, and the election was really never in doubt. In addition to his solid support in the South, Jefferson made significant inroads in once-solid Federalist New England through his actions during his first term of office as president.

3. The outcome of the election was not even close, with Jefferson winning by a vote in the electoral college of 162 to Pinkney's 14 votes! Jefferson's engineering of the Louisiana Purchase was not only his most significant achievement, but it literally doubled the size of the United States. In the space below, outline the deal Jefferson cut with Napoleon in what probably was the greatest real estate deal of all time!

   _____

   _____

   _____

   _____

   _____

JAMES MADISON

★★★★★★★★★★★★★★★★★★★★★★★★★★

James Madison was the smallest of our presidents, standing only 5'4" and weighing only 100 pounds. But his accomplishments made him a better-than-average president, according to a 1962 poll of 75 historians conducted by Arthur M. Schlesinger, Sr., who ranked the first 31 presidents. Historically, his greatest accomplishment was the distinction of being designated the "Father of the Constitution."

Madison was born on March 16, 1751, at the home of his grandparents in King George County, Virginia. His early education included intense study under Donald Robertson, whom Madison later credited as the "greatest influence on his education." Unlike most of his peers who enrolled at William and Mary, Madison chose the College of New Jersey (now Princeton), where he studied Latin, Greek, science, and the other main courses of study within a college curriculum. After graduation, Madison remained at Princeton to study Hebrew and philosophy. He studied law sporadically but was never admitted to the bar.

His political career began as a member of the Virginia House of Delegates in 1776. He then became a member of the Council of State, which was followed by his election to the Continental Congress in 1780. In 1784 he was again chosen as a member of the Virginia House of Delegates, where he fiercely defended his belief in separation of church and state. In 1786 he was chosen as a delegate to the Annapolis Convention that eventually led to the Constitutional Convention. He drafted much of the document through the use of his copious notes and their interpretation. He was elected to the U.S. House of Representatives in 1789 and then became Thomas Jefferson's secretary of state in 1801. He supported the purchase of the Louisiana Territory and vehemently denounced the impressment of American sailors on the high seas by the British.

ELECTION OF 1808
The Republicans were for the first time divided over their choice for president. Thomas Jefferson, elected twice, had the nomination for the asking. But he chose to retire and openly favored Madison. But there was support within the party for George Clinton of New York and James Monroe of Virginia. Madison was eventually chosen as the candidate with Clinton as the choice for vice president. The Federalists again chose Charles Cotesworth Pinckney with Rufus King as their vice-presidential candidate.

1. James Madison was vulnerable on only one important issue in the election of 1808. During his tenure as secretary of state, he had supported an embargo against Britain and France to respect American neutrality. Why was this embargo unpopular in the United States, and why did the Federalists seize the opportunity to discredit Madison because of it?

   _____

   _____

2. With the Federalist party briefly "revitalized" over the embargo issue, members campaigned vigorously for their candidate, Charles Cotesworth Pinckney. In the space below, create two campaign slogans the Federalists might have used during the campaign of 1808.

   _____

   _____

ELECTION OF 1812

James Madison easily won the election of 1808 and thus was renominated unanimously by Republican congressmen as their candidate for president in the election of 1812. Elbridge Gerry of Massachusetts was chosen as the Republican candidate for vice president. DeWitt Clinton, nephew of George Clinton (Madison's first vice president) was the very popular mayor of New York, and state legislators from New York wanted him to run for president. When the Federalists declined to nominate a candidate, Clinton was assured overwhelming support by the Federalists. Jared Ingersoll was chosen as the vice-presidential nominee.

3. The War of 1812 was the dominating issue of this campaign. The country was as politically divided over the war as it was over the two candidates who were running. Research the background of the War of 1812 and indicate the political stance maintained by each of the candidates.

   _____

   _____

   _____

4. Although Madison won the election, the electoral vote was much closer than when Madison was first elected in 1808. Find out the results of the electoral vote and record them in the space below.

   _____

   _____

5. Find out why the Battle of New Orleans that ended the War of 1812 would never have been fought today. Record your answer on the back.

JAMES MONROE

★ ★

It was during the two administrations of James Monroe (1817–1825) that America experienced what came to be known as the "era of good feelings." During this brief period in American history, a single party commanded the affections of virtually all segments of the society, and it was no doubt the lack of partisan struggle that was most responsible for this feeling.

Monroe was born on April 28, 1758, in Westmoreland County, Virginia, the son of a prosperous Virginia planter. His father died when he was 16. Monroe considered his mother among the "most educated women in Virginia," but little else is known about her. His early education included study at Campbelltown Academy, and he enrolled at the College of William and Mary when he was 16. The prospect of revolution in the colonies caused him to drop out of college in 1775 and join a band of older men who raided the British arsenal at the Governor's Palace. Monroe then joined the Continental Army and never returned to college to earn his degree.

He served the military well, rising to the rank of major by the time of the Revolution. Thomas Jefferson rewarded his brilliant military record by appointing him military commissioner of Virginia. His political career began in 1782 as a member of the Virginia Assembly. He was then elected to three terms in the Continental Congress. In 1790 he was elected to the United States Senate, where he became the chief lieutenant of Thomas Jefferson. President Washington later appointed him as minister to France, but he was recalled by Washington for failure to "actively defend Jay's Treaty with Great Britain." Monroe was elected governor of Virginia and led the campaign in 1800 to elect Thomas Jefferson as president. He served as one of the envoys who negotiated the Louisiana Purchase and was appointed by President Jefferson as minister to Great Britain. He served as secretary of state under President Madison and in 1814 began a dual role in Madison's cabinet by also becoming the secretary of war.

ELECTION OF 1816
The accomplishments of his successful political background and support from both Jefferson and Madison made him the heir apparent to become president in 1816. Both former presidents supported his nomination, and he received only token competition from William Crawford, who in the end failed to even declare himself a candidate because he was so convinced of inevitable defeat by Monroe. The Republican choice for vice president was Daniel D. Tompkins of New York. Rufus King had run unsuccessfully twice on the Federalist ticket with Charles Cotesworth Pinckney in the elections of 1804 and 1808. He was perhaps the strongest of the few remaining Federalists, and they supported him, but they never formally nominated him as their candidate. John Howard of Maryland emerged as the chief Federalist candidate for vice president.

1. The Federalist Party had been on the downslide since the election of John Adams in 1796, but the War of 1812 virtually brought on the party's demise. Research the Federalist position on the War of 1812 and how the outcome brought an end to the Federalists as a party.

_____

_____

_____

ELECTION OF 1820

Monroe's renomination was such a foregone conclusion that very few Republicans bothered to attend the nominating caucus. Rather than nominate Monroe with only a few votes, the caucus decided not to make a formal nomination. Thus Monroe and his vice president (Daniel D. Tompkins) became de facto candidates for reelection. There was no opposition mounted against them. Not since George Washington had a president enjoyed such broadbased support. Even former President John Adams, a strong Federalist, came out of retirement and, as an elector in Massachusetts, supported Monroe. It was indeed an "Era of Good Feelings."

2. In the actual electoral vote Monroe received 231 of the 232 electoral votes. Find out who cast the single vote against Monroe by voting for Secretary of State John Quincy Adams. What were the reasons for casting the dissenting vote?

_____

_____

_____

3. One of the important pieces of legislation passed during the administration of James Monroe was the Missouri Compromise of 1820. Find out the significance of the legislation and the position of President Monroe and record your findings in the space below.

_____

_____

_____

4. In 1823 Monroe laid down what was to become the cornerstone of American foreign policy for the rest of the nineteenth century. It became known as the Monroe Doctrine. Explain in the space below and on the back of this sheet what the Monroe Doctrine meant to the rest of the world.

_____

_____

_____

_____

JOHN QUINCY ADAMS

★ ★

John Quincy Adams was almost completely bald by the time he became president. He had penetrating black eyes and he dressed plainly, without care. By his own admission, he described his shortcomings as a ". . . man of reserved, cold, austere and forbidding manners. My political adversaries regard me as a gloomy misanthropist, my personal enemies as an unsocial savage. With a knowledge of this defect in my personality, I have not the pliability to reform it!"

Adams was born in 1767 in Braintree, Massachusetts, the son of John Adams, the second president of the United States. He remains the only son of a president to become president. His mother, Abigail, remains the only wife of a president who was also the mother of a president. Adams was truly a child of the Revolution, as he grew up amid more excitement than perhaps any other president. He and his mother witnessed the Battle of Bunker Hill from a vantage point on a hill not far away. With his father deeply involved in the Revolution, Adams was always concerned about his family's safety and their future.

He received his early education in Paris schools while his father served there as a diplomat. He later returned to the United States and followed in his father's footsteps by enrolling at Harvard Law School, and he was admitted to the bar in 1790. He opened a law office in Boston but found very few clients. His political career began with his appointment as a diplomat to the Netherlands by President Washington. In 1797 Washington appointed him as minister to Prussia. After his return to the United States, he was elected to the Massachusetts state senate. He later became a U.S. senator and then was appointed by President Madison as the first U.S. minister to Russia. After the War of 1812, Madison again called on Adams to head the American negotiating team during the Treaty of Ghent that ended the war. Adams began a tenure as the minister to Great Britain in 1815 and in 1817 was appointed by President Monroe as secretary of state.

ELECTION OF 1824

The year 1824 was a time when the practice of the nominating caucus was being perceived as a less-than-satisfactory method of choosing presidential candidates. But it was also a time prior to the emergence of national political conventions as we know them today. It was more or less a case of regional endorsements, and the Massachusetts legislature formally nominated Adams in February of 1824. The rest of New England quickly followed suit. The Kentucky legislature had already nominated Henry Clay. The Tennessee legislature nominated Andrew Jackson, and several other states in the West supported him as well. Secretary of the Treasury William C. Crawford became a fourth candidate for president, though he received no formal endorsement from any state legislature.

1. The campaign turned into a battle of sectional rivalries and eventually became focused on the personalities of the four candidates. Find out in which section of the nation each candidate found his greatest support and record your findings in the space below.

   _____

   _____

   _____

2. Research the election results and record the popular vote and the vote of the electoral college in the space below.

	POPULAR VOTE	ELECTORAL VOTE
John Quincy Adams	_____	_____
Andrew Jackson	_____	_____
Henry Clay	_____	_____
William H. Crawford	_____	_____

3. Look at the results above. According to the electoral vote, Jackson should have become president. What directive in the Constitution prevented him from being named president of the United States following the election?

   _____

   _____

   _____

   _____

4. What was the outcome of the vote that placed John Quincy Adams in the White House? How was Adams able to win even though he had not won the popular vote nor had he won the greatest number of electoral votes? Explain how Adams was still able to win the presidency, despite the election results.

   _____

   _____

   _____

   _____

5. What was the reaction of Andrew Jackson to the result?

   _____

   _____

ANDREW JACKSON

★ ★

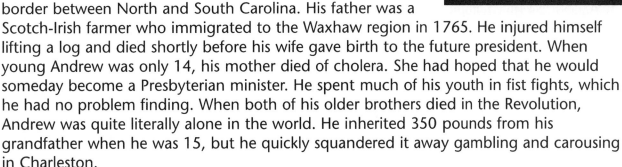

Courtesy Metropolitan Museum of Art, Dick Fund

Andrew Jackson was tall and lean (6 feet, 1 inch tall and weighed only 140 pounds) and suffered from poor health most of his adult life. He often used a cane to steady his faltering gait. Jackson was quick-tempered and thin-skinned, but he also had a charismatic charm about him that made him quite popular with people.

Jackson was born in 1767 in the Waxhaw region on the border between North and South Carolina. His father was a Scotch-Irish farmer who immigrated to the Waxhaw region in 1765. He injured himself lifting a log and died shortly before his wife gave birth to the future president. When young Andrew was only 14, his mother died of cholera. She had hoped that he would someday become a Presbyterian minister. He spent much of his youth in fist fights, which he had no problem finding. When both of his older brothers died in the Revolution, Andrew was quite literally alone in the world. He inherited 350 pounds from his grandfather when he was 15, but he quickly squandered it away gambling and carousing in Charleston.

Although his mother had wanted him to become a minister, young Andrew had no desire for the clergy. He taught school for one year and later decided on pursuing a career as a lawyer. In 1787 he was admitted to the North Carolina bar. When he was 24, he married Rachel Donelson Robards. Although she was divorced, a technicality in the law nullified the marriage for a time, even though the Jacksons were not aware of the problem. They remarried once her divorce became official, but the scandal that followed during Jackson's bid for the presidency haunted her to an early death.

Jackson was more famous for his military record than his political background when he ran for president. During the War of 1812, Jackson was appointed a major general of the U.S. Volunteers in Tennessee. His reputation as an Indian fighter grew to be a legend. After several victories over the Creek Indians in Florida, Jackson went to New Orleans, where he defended the city against the British. He helped deliver a final stunning defeat (The Battle of New Orleans) in which more than 2,000 British troops were killed. Only 21 Americans died in that famous battle that ended the War of 1812, even though the Treaty of Ghent had already been signed. Jackson did have a political background (having served as a U.S. representative and a U.S. senator), but it was his record as a war hero that propelled him into the presidency.

ELECTION OF 1828

Jackson was so bitter about the election of 1824, in which he won both the popular vote and the electoral vote (yet lost the election in the House of Representatives), that he decided almost immediately to run for president in 1828. He was nominated by the Tennessee state legislature. Jackson's supporters called themselves *Democrats*. Thus began the transformation of Jeffersonian Republicans into the modern-day Democratic party. John Quincy Adams' supporters called themselves National Republicans. The campaign centered around the personalities of the two men. Adams was the more polished and experienced politician, and Jackson was the war hero who represented the democratic spirit that was so much a part of the West and the South.

1. Andrew Jackson's running mate for vice president was John C. Calhoun of South Carolina, the vice president under incumbent John Quincy Adams. How did having Calhoun on the Democratic ticket help Jackson win the election for president in 1828?

   _____

   _____

2. The election of 1828 signaled the emergence of the Democratic and Republican parties as we know them today. In the space below describe how the two parties emerged and the main difference in their political beliefs at this early stage.

   _____

   _____

ELECTION OF 1832

This was the first presidential election in which the candidates were chosen at national party conventions. The Democrats chose Jackson as their presidential candidate and reluctantly endorsed Jackson's choice of Martin Van Buren as their candidate for vice president. The National Republicans chose Henry Clay as their candidate for president and nominated John Sergeant of Pennsylvania as their candidate for vice president.

3. Among the campaign issues was criticism by Clay and the National Republicans of Jackson's use of the "spoils system." Find out the meaning of this term and Jackson's response to those who criticized his endorsement of it.

   _____

   _____

4. Andrew Jackson became famous for his Kitchen Cabinet. Find out how this term originated and what this group of men meant to Jackson.

   _____

   _____

MARTIN VAN BUREN

★ ★

Martin Van Buren stood only 5 feet 6 inches tall and had deeply set blue eyes and a classic Roman nose. By the time he became president, he was distinguished by unruly white hair and great sidewhiskers. His personal charm and fine manners plus his impeccable dress and natty appearance made him a much-sought-after party guest. Van Buren was also an engaging conversationalist who was well known for his ability to draw out the feelings of others but keep his own opinions to himself. He was as different from Andrew Jackson as night from day, but he always remained loyal to Jackson (he always considered him a true friend), who was perhaps most responsible for his election to the presidency.

Van Buren was born in 1782 at Kinderhook, New York. He was the first president born an American citizen, since all his predecessors had been born prior to the Declaration of Independence and were thus considered British subjects. His father was a farmer and tavern keeper, and "Little Mat," as the future president was called, spent much of his childhood helping his father in the tavern after school. He often listened quietly to the political conversations that took place there.

At the age of 14, he began studying law under Francis Sylvester, who saw real potential in Van Buren as a promising attorney. By the age of 15, Sylvester entrusted Van Buren to sum up his first case to present to a jury. Six years later he was admitted to the bar. His political career began with his election to the New York State Senate, where he gained a reputation as a very influential politician. In 1821 he was elected to the U.S. Senate. During the election of 1828, he campaigned vigorously for Andrew Jackson and helped to forge a North-South alliance that led to Jackson's victory. Van Buren then ran successfully for governor of New York. Some say he ran only to improve Jackson's chances of winning that state in his race for the presidency. He resigned shorty after election to the governorship to become Jackson's secretary of state. Van Buren exerted great influence within the administration and often encouraged Jackson to take full advantage of the spoils system. As the only member of the cabinet to obey Jackson's orders, he became a close friend to the president and a trusted member of his Kitchen Cabinet.

In the election of 1832, he became Jackson's choice as the Democratic vice-presidential candidate. However, there was much opposition to Van Buren within the Democratic party. In the end the party reluctantly bowed to Jackson's wishes and nominated Van Buren. Jackson wanted Van Buren as his vice president because he felt that would put Van Buren in an excellent position to win the presidency in 1836. While Jackson was in office, Van Buren always supported his decisions, even though he did not always agree with the president.

ELECTION OF 1836

Jackson's strategy paid off as the Democrats unanimously nominated Van Buren on the first ballot as their choice for president. Richard M. Johnson of Kentucky was chosen as the vice-presidential candidate. Johnson was also Jackson's hand-picked choice. Opposition was provided by a new party called the *Whigs*. The party emerged out of hatred for Andrew Jackson, whom they referred to as King Andrew I. Their strategy was to have a candidate for president in each region of the country, with the hope of denying Van Buren a majority and thus throwing the election into the House of Representatives. Their candidate in the West was William Henry Harrison; in the Northeast their choice was Daniel Webster; and the Whig candidate in the South was Hugh Lawson White.

1. Van Buren's main objective was to maintain a coalition of northern and southern political machinery that had been the basis of strength in the Jacksonian years. To do this, he needed to satisfy North and South alike. One of the issues was whether or not Congress had the power to abolish slavery in the nation's capital. How did Van Buren handle this issue during his campaign?

   _____
   _____
   _____

2. The election of 1836 was unusual because no fewer than five candidates actually won electoral votes. Research the results of the election and record the names of the candidates and the votes they won in the electoral college.

   _____
   _____

3. Another unusual aspect of the election of 1836 was the election of the vice president. Find out the circumstances surrounding this one-of-a-kind election and record your answer in the space below.

   _____
   _____
   _____

4. Go back to your answer for question #2. Add together all of the electoral votes of all the candidates. How many electoral votes were cast? Look at the Twelfth Amendment to the Constitution. Find out how many electoral votes Virginia had and how many Johnson would have needed to avoid the election being sent to the U.S. Senate. Who finally won the election for vice president? Record your response below.

   _____
   _____
   _____
   _____

WILLIAM HENRY HARRISON

★ ★

He was described as good-humored, affable, and very accessible. William Henry Harrison was characterized as a plainspoken man of average height, with thin brown hair which he combed carelessly straight down over his forehead. He had a long, thin face distinguished by a long, sharp-bridged nose, closely set eyes, thin lips, and a strong jaw. Harrison has the rather unfortunate distinction of having served as this country's president for a shorter period of time than any other president.

He was born in 1773 at Berkeley plantation, Charles City County, Virginia. He was the last president to be born a British subject. His father, Benjamin Harrison V, was a politician who distinguished himself by being a member of the Continental Congress, by being one of the signers of the Declaration of Independence, and by being governor of Virginia. Not much is known about his mother, who was named Elizabeth. William Henry was the youngest of seven children.

Harrison grew up as a child of the American Revolution. Hessian troops once raided his family's home at Berkeley, stripping the house of its furnishings and slaughtering all the livestock. Young William Henry and his family learned in advance of the attack, so they were able to escape to safety. At a young age, he decided he wanted to become a doctor. Much of his early education was on the plantation, but he later served an apprenticeship in Richmond before enrolling in the Pennsylvania Medical School in Philadelphia. When his father died and the money ran out, he dropped out of medical school and joined the army.

William Henry Harrison's career before the presidency was one of both military and political service. He was a professional soldier with impressive credentials dating back to the Indian wars in the Northwest Territory during the 1790s. He served as secretary of the Northwest Territory under President John Adams, then later became a Northwest Territory delegate for the U.S. House. He was later appointed governor of the Indiana Territory and served in that capacity for 12 years under Presidents Adams, Jefferson, and Madison. During that time he negotiated a number of treaties with the Indians. When the treaties were not honored, he sometimes led the troops himself. One of his most famous military accomplishments was called the Battle of Tippecanoe.

During the War of 1812, he served as brigadier general in command of the Northwest Territory. As the head of 2,100 Kentucky volunteers, 200 friendly Indians, and 120 other volunteers, he soundly defeated a force of 1,700 British troops and unfriendly Indians. His victory at the Battle of the Thames secured the Northwest and made Harrison a national hero. He then became a member of the U.S. House of Representatives, later an Ohio state senator, then a U.S. senator, and after that the minister to Colombia. He unsuccessfully ran for president in 1836 against Martin Van Buren.

ELECTION OF 1840

Harrison was a member of the emerging party called Whigs, who were desperately wanting to place a man in the White House. During their party convention in 1839, the front-running candidate appeared to be Henry Clay. As the convention wore on, Harrison began to gain ground and in the end was chosen as the Whig Party candidate. Its chosen candidate for vice president was John Tyler. The Democratic Party unanimously nominated President Martin Van Buren. Opposition to Vice President Richard M. Johnson had grown to the point that the party refused to endorse him, so he ran as a de facto nominee.

1. During the campaign a Democratic newspaper in Baltimore attempted to belittle Harrison by characterizing him as a frontier hick who drank hard cider and lived in a log cabin. Research this campaign and find out how the strategy behind the campaign by the Democrats backfired and how the story actually turned into a plus for the Whigs and Harrison.

   _____

   _____

   _____

   _____

2. The slogan that caught on for the Whigs during the campaign of 1840 was "Tippecanoe and Tyler, too." Find out the significance of this campaign slogan that was used to build a positive image for Harrison and the Whig Party among undecided voters.

   _____

   _____

   _____

3. The Democratic Party produced the first national party platform during this campaign of 1840. In the space below list what the party hoped to accomplish if voters would restore Martin Van Buren (their candidate) to another term as president.

   _____

   _____

4. While the Whig Party did not draft a platform, it was quick to criticize that of the Democrats. What was the Whigs' greatest criticism of what had happened during Van Buren's first term, an event that most likely led to Van Buren's stunning defeat for reelection in 1840?

   _____

   _____

   _____

JOHN TYLER

John Tyler became the first man to become our nation's president without being elected. Even though Tyler was not an elected president, his tenure in office included events that were significant to the story of America. Tyler was a tall, thin man of dignified charm who typified the mannerisms of a well-bred Southerner during the nineteenth century.

He was born in 1790 at Greenway, the family plantation on the James River in Charles County, Virginia. His father, who eventually became a governor of Virginia and finally a U.S. circuit judge, was a planter with over 40 slaves. Not much is known about young John Tyler's mother, as she died when he was only seven years old.

At the age of 12, Tyler enrolled in the preparatory division of the College of William and Mary in Williamsburg. He progressed to the college level and graduated when he was only 17 years old. He then studied law with his cousin Samuel Tyler and with Edmund Randolph and was admitted to the bar in 1809. Tyler was an accomplished violin player as well as being an expert marksman and good hunter. He first married Letitia Christian and with her he had four daughters and three sons. When she died after a 29-year happy marriage, Tyler married Julia Gardner, who was 30 years younger than the 54-year-old Tyler. By his second wife, Tyler had five sons and two daughters, giving him a total of 14 children to live to maturity—more than any other president.

Tyler's career before the presidency included a brief and rather uneventful tour of duty during the War of 1812. His political background included being elected on three different occasions as a member of the Virginia House of Delegates. He was also elected to two terms in the U.S. House of Representatives and was later elected to the U.S. Senate.

1. As a delegate to the Whig National Convention in Harrisburg, Pennsylvania, in 1839, Tyler was in support of Henry Clay. Find out why Tyler was eventually chosen as the vice-presidential candidate to run on the Whig ticket with William Henry Harrison, even though Tyler had supported Clay during the convention.

   _____

   _____

2. As the first person to accede to the presidency on the death of the president, Tyler began his term amid great controversy. The Constitution was ambiguous on the right of succession. How did Tyler pave the way for future vice presidents who were to be elevated to the status of president?

   _____

   _____

   _____

3. When William Henry Harrison died in office shortly after becoming president, John Tyler retained all of Harrison's cabinet members. However, within a short period of time, all members of the cabinet resigned with the exception of Daniel Webster. What caused this mass resignation?

_____

_____

4. Why was John Tyler regarded as a "president without a party"?

_____

_____

5. In early 1844 President Tyler approved the treaty for the annexation of Texas. Why were Tyler and the South so anxious to annex Texas when such action appeared to create definite trouble ahead with Mexico?

_____

_____

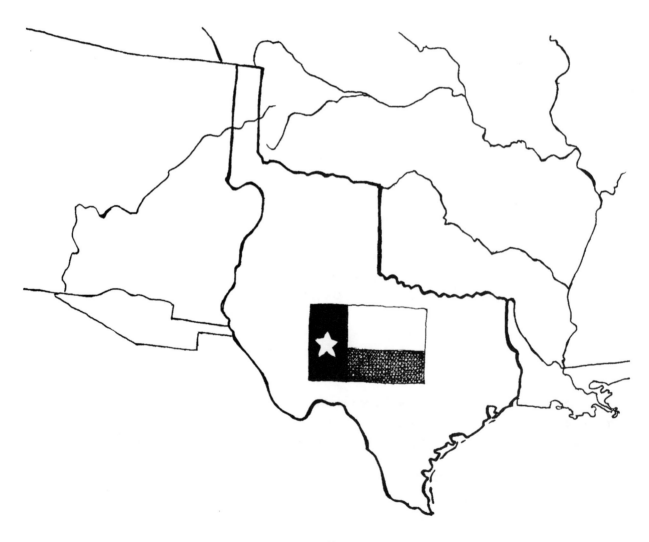

JAMES POLK

★ ★

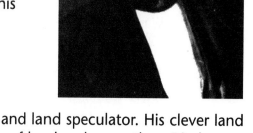

James Polk was a classic example of an overachiever. His ambition has been traced to a childhood in which he drove himself ruthlessly to exploit the abilities he did have to make up for those areas where he was not strong. This driving ambition carried through to his presidency, highlighted by the dramatic expansion of the United States that occurred during his administration.

Polk was born in 1795 in Mecklensburg County, North Carolina. His father was a prosperous planter, surveyor, and land speculator. His clever land deals eventually brought him to own thousands of acres of land and more than 50 slaves. Polk's mother outlived many of her children, including the president.

Much of young Jimmy Polk's early education was informal, but by the time he had reached the age of 21, he had enrolled at the University of North Carolina. He was an excellent student, and after he graduated from college, he decided to pursue a career in politics. To that end he began to study law, and by 1820 he was admitted to the bar.

His career prior to the presidency began with his election to the Tennessee House of Representatives. He followed that with election to the U.S. House of Representatives. Polk was reelected to the House six times in succession. During that tenure in the House, he was chosen Speaker of the House for two terms. Polk then became the governor of Tennessee. He tried unsuccessfully to win the Democratic vice-presidential nomination in 1840.

ELECTION OF 1844

Former President Martin Van Buren appeared to be the logical choice when the Democratic convention began. But Van Buren was unable to gain the necessary two-thirds margin required to win the nomination. By the ninth ballot the convention threw its support behind James Polk, and he was awarded the nomination. Because he was such an underdog, he was considered a "dark-horse" candidate. His vice-presidential running mate was Silas Wright. Polk's opponent was the Whig candidate Henry Clay, and Theodore Frelinghuysen of New Jersey was nominated as the Whig Party's vice-presidential candidate.

1. Both parties drafted platforms as the candidates began to campaign for the election of 1844. Research the issues that were supported by each candidate and indicate whether each plank below would be a part of the Democratic (D) Party platform or the Whig (W) Party platform:

_____ Supported the annexation of Texas

_____ Supported a well-regulated currency

_____ Wanted to limit presidents to serving a single term of office

_____ Was against any federally funded internal improvements

_____ Was against any federal interference with slavery issue

_____ Supported high tariffs

_____ Was opposed to the resurrection of the Bank of the United States of America

_____ Supported distribution of proceeds from the sale of public lands

2. When the campaign began, most people thought that Henry Clay would have little trouble beating the dark-horse candidate, James Polk. Find out how Clay hurt his own chances and allowed Polk to win the election.

_____

_____

_____

3. James Polk was the first dark-horse candidate to win the nomination for president from a major party. He was also the first dark-horse candidate to win the presidency. Define the term *dark-horse candidate* and tell why a major party would choose to run such a person for president.

_____

_____

_____

4. James Polk is considered historically to have been one of our nation's most important presidents because of the expansion of the boundaries of the United States that occurred during his administration. Choose one of the following for further research and report your findings on the back of this sheet:

   a. The implications and results of his party's cry for "Fifty-four Forty or Fight!"

   b. The implications and results of the popular philosophy in America at the time called "Manifest Destiny."

ZACHARY TAYLOR

★ ★

Zachary Taylor will always be remembered as a war hero who became president. His sloppy and careless manner of dress combined with his occasional problem of stammering when speaking in public led many to characterize him mistakenly as an ill-mannered boor, which was indeed far from the truth. In fact, Taylor was a very gracious gentleman, even to the point of gallantry where women were concerned.

Taylor's father, Richard Taylor, was a planter and public official who moved his family from Virginia to Louisville, Kentucky, in 1784. Over the years he acquired more than 10,000 acres of land in various parts of Kentucky. Not much is known of Taylor's mother except that her hands were permanently disfigured in an accident while she was making bullets.

Zachary Taylor was born in 1784 in Orange County, Virginia. Young Zachary received only the most basic education and he remained a poor speller throughout his entire life. He preferred the company of friends to any kind of physical recreation, although he was a good swimmer. He did not smoke, but he did chew tobacco, and he developed a reputation as an unusually skilled marksman with a spittoon.

Unlike most of the other early presidents who had political backgrounds, Taylor was a career military man. His career spanned nearly 40 years in which he rose from the rank of first lieutenant to that of major general. He started in the Seventh Infantry Regiment in 1808, then distinguished himself with a meritorious service record during the War of 1812, the Blackhawk War, the Second Seminole War, and finally the Mexican War. In exchange for the Mexicans surrendering to him the city of Monterrey, he allowed them to leave the city with their firearms and promised not to pursue them for six weeks. When President James Polk found out about this, he was furious and stripped Taylor of most of his troops, putting them under the command of General Winfield Scott.

Taylor vowed to continue doing the best he could with the troops that remained under his command. During a fierce battle with Santa Ana at Buena Vista, he narrowly escaped death twice, and his army suffered only one-third the casualties that were inflicted on the Mexican Army. When Santa Ana was forced to withdraw, Taylor became a national hero.

ELECTION OF 1848
At the Whig convention in Philadelphia, Taylor was the overwhelming choice. Their party platform consisted of praising Taylor's virtues and embellishing his military record. Millard Fillmore was chosen as his running mate. The Democratic nomination went to Lewis Cass of Michigan, while his running mate became William O. Butler.

1. Zachary Taylor was 64 years old, had never been involved in politics before, knew next to nothing about national issues, and had never even voted! Daniel Webster called him "an illiterate frontier colonel." Despite all this, he still won the nomination? How?

_____

_____

_____

2. The dominant issue of the campaign was slavery, particularly the Wilmot Proviso. Find out about the Wilmot Proviso. What was it? How did Zachary Taylor feel about it? What was the position of his opponent, the Democratic candidate Lewis Cass?

_____

_____

_____

_____

_____

3. How did third-party candidate former president Martin Van Buren help Taylor win the election?

_____

_____

_____

MILLARD FILLMORE

★ ★

"Secondhand . . . commonplace . . . mediocre . . . undistinguished," are the words that historians have used to analyze Millard Fillmore's brief rise from obscurity and his quick descent into oblivion. He was a likable fellow and a very practical man who relied on logic and common sense to make his point. His meager beginnings gave him a focus and determination early in life to improve his livelihood and become successful. In his brief time as president filling out the term of Zachary Taylor, he served his country as best he could, but historians who rank our presidents have placed him near the bottom of almost every list in "importance" and "significance."

He was born in Locke Township, Cayuga County, New York, in 1800. His father was a farmer who tried without much success in Vermont and later in various places in New York. After struggling as a tenant farmer, he finally moved his family to Aurora, near Buffalo, New York. Millard Fillmore was named after his mother, Phoebe Millard Fillmore.

As a youth he helped his father to clear the land, plow fields, and harvest the meager crops. Fillmore did not like farming at all, so his father apprenticed him to a clothmaker when he was only 14 years old. Young Millard did not like that occupation either. He received very little education until he was 17, when he developed a love of reading, but he realized that he did not understand much of what he read because of his lack of education. He later enrolled at an academy, where his teacher was Abigail

Powers. The two developed a loving relationship and Fillmore later married her. Millard Fillmore studied law in Buffalo at the offices of friends until he finally passed the bar exam in 1823.

Fillmore's career prior to becoming president included service as a New York state assemblyman, followed by election to Congress as a Whig representative from western New York. He was re-elected to Congress three times. In 1844 he was a candidate for the Whig Party nomination for vice president but was defeated by Silas Wright. He then became comptroller of New York, and in 1848 he won the Whig Party nomination for vice president on the ticket with Zachary Taylor.

1. Prior to the national convention of the Whig Party in 1848, Millard Fillmore and Zachary Taylor had never met! In fact, they never did meet until after the election of 1848. Fillmore was largely ignored by the Taylor administration. Find out how he used his power as presiding officer of the Senate to respond to the Taylor administration.

_____

_____

_____

_____

_____

_____

2. When Zachary Taylor died in office in 1850, Millard Fillmore was elevated to the presidency. He reversed the policy of Taylor, who had opposed the Compromise of 1850, and embraced it as a way of avoiding civil war. Research the Compromise of 1850 and list the provisions of this important legislation that helped to avert civil war, at least for a time.

_____

_____

_____

_____

_____

_____

_____

3. Find out the importance of the mission which President Fillmore sent Commodore Matthew Perry on and the impact it had on American trade.

_____

_____

_____

_____

_____

_____

_____

_____

_____

_____

FRANKLIN PIERCE

★★★★★★★★★★★★★★★★★★★★★★★★★

Franklin Pierce was America's second dark-horse candidate to become president of the United States. He was one of our nation's most handsome presidents with dark, curly hair, a classic Roman nose, gray eyes, and thin lips. His health was generally not good, as he often suffered from respiratory ailments, chronic bronchitis, bouts of severe depression, and a severe problem with alcoholism. History has not been kind in its assessment of Pierce as a president.

He was born in 1804 in a log cabin on the Contoocook River near Hillsborough, New Hampshire. His father had fought in the American Revolution and later served in various capacities as a public official. Franklin Pierce had a deep affection for his mother, but from her he unfortunately inherited many of his illnesses. As a young boy, Pierce was a bright student who dearly loved school. After studying at Hancock Academy, he enrolled at Bowdoin College in Brunswick, Maine. There he became close friends with Nathaniel Hawthorne. After graduating, he pursued a career in law and in 1827 was admitted to the bar.

Pierce's career prior to the presidency included military service during the Mexican War. He was injured twice during battle and on both occasions he fainted. After the war he was elected to the New Hampshire state legislature. His next political move was successful election to the House of Representatives. After being elected for another term, he ran for election to the United States Senate. For a number of political reasons including the unhealthy atmosphere of Washington, D.C., Pierce resigned from his seat in the Senate in 1842.

ELECTION OF 1852
When the Democratic Party gathered for its national convention in early 1852, the leading candidate for the nomination was Lewis Cass. Second in the running was James Buchanan, followed by Stephen Douglas of Illinois and William Marcey. As the balloting wore on, one candidate would surface . . . then another . . . but no one could get enough votes to get the margin necessary to win the nomination. On the thirty-fifth ballot, the name of Franklin Pierce first appeared and, by the forty-ninth ballot, he had gathered enough strength to win the nomination almost unanimously. William R. King was nominated as the Democratic vice-presidential candidate.

1. The Whig Party nominated war hero Winfield Scott, whose name had been thrust into national prominence following his heroics in the Mexican War. He won the nomination over incumbent president Millard Fillmore. William A. Graham was nominated for vice president. The campaign slogan for the Democratic Party became "We Polked You in 1844; We Shall Pierce You in 1852!" What do you think is the significance of this slogan and what does it mean?

   _____

   _____

   _____

2. Pierce was known as a "doughface"—a Northern man with Southern principles. Find out about his feelings on slavery and how Pierce regarded the abolitionist movement and record your answer in the space below.

   _____

   _____

   _____

3. The campaign of 1852 became one of each party downgrading the other party's candidate. Find out how the election marked the end of the Whig Party.

   _____

   _____

   _____

JAMES BUCHANAN

★ ★

James Buchanan was an imposing, handsome figure with many friends and scruples that were beyond reproach. He was a man of strong family ties and possessed a forgiving temper. He carried himself with an air of dignity and grace that made him popular wherever he went. His most distinctive physical feature was his wryneck, which was caused by a peculiar eye disorder. One eye was farsighted; the other was nearsighted. He also had one eyeball pitched higher than the other. To compensate for this, he often cocked his head and closed one eye. He was and remains today the only president to never marry. Historians rank him near the very bottom in his performance as president.

James Buchanan was another of the log cabin presidents, being born in 1791 at Cove Gap near Mercersburg, Pennsylvania. His father was a reasonably successful merchant and farmer; his mother was a woman who strongly believed in education, to the point of regularly testing her children's powers of reason. James Buchanan attributed to her all responsibility for his success.

In school, Buchanan was a good student but one who seemed prone to getting into trouble. When he was a student at Dickinson College, he was asked not to come back the next year because of his conduct. His father's good name kept him in school and, from that point on, Buchanan applied himself diligently. He became interested in the study of law and was admitted to the bar in 1812.

Buchanan's political career began with his election to the Pennsylvania House of Representatives. His next step was election, then reelection three times, to the U.S. House of Representatives. He served as the U.S. minister to Russia under the Andrew Jackson administration and three terms as a U.S. senator before becoming James Polk's secretary of state. Finally, he was President Franklin Pierce's minister to Great Britain.

ELECTION OF 1856

By the time the Democrats convened in 1856, Buchanan had all the credentials to be the front-runner for the nomination for president. His popularity exceeded that of both President Franklin Pierce and Senator Stephen Douglas of Illinois. By the seventeenth ballot, Buchanan was the unanimous choice for the nomination. The vice-presidential nomination went to John C. Breckinridge. The Republicans nominated John C. Fremont for president, and his running mate became William L. Dayton of New Jersey.

1. The Republican campaign slogan was "Free Speech, Free Press, Free Soil, Free Man, Fremont, and Victory!" What implications would this slogan have had on the slave owners in the South?

   _____

   _____

2. While the election was reasonably close, Buchanan won all three of the key states that were considered "very close" (Illinois, Indiana, and Pennsylvania). The results were Buchanan, 174; Fremont, 114; and former president Millard Fillmore (of the Know-Nothing and Whig Parties) only eight electoral votes. When Buchanan entered the White House, he felt that he could quiet the storm over slavery. Why was this only an illusion?

   _____

   What was Buchanan's position on each of the following?

   slavery _____

   _____

   Fugitive Slave Act _____

   _____

   Dred Scott decision _____

   _____

3. Although James Buchanan never married, he was considered to be a very handsome man and he carried with him an air of a refined gentleman. Find out why he never got married.

   _____

   _____

   _____

   _____

   _____

   _____

   _____

   _____

   _____

   _____

ABRAHAM LINCOLN

★ ★

History ranks him as one of our greatest presidents, yet while he was in office he was vilified from all sides. Abolitionists, states'-righters, strict constructionists, radicals, conservatives, and armchair strategists all found their bones to pick with him. There were those who just did not like his looks and ridiculed his gangly body and homely face. Historians agree that no other president before or since has faced more difficult times. He countered his sadness and despair with a sense of humor that was a delightful mixture of dry wit, satire, and timely, well-chosen remarks and stories.

Abraham Lincoln was born on February 12, 1809, in a dirt-floored, one-room cabin near Hodgenville, Kentucky. His father was a carpenter and farmer. His mother died of milk sickness when Abraham was only nine years old. Young Lincoln spent much of his childhood helping his father by splitting wood and clearing the land. He did not have a close relationship with his father and did not even attend the funeral when his father died. Lincoln estimated that the total of his formal education was less than a single year. He had an intense passion for reading, however, and he read anything he could get his hands on. His stepmother supported his love for reading and provided him with books whenever she could. He spent hours and hours reading the family Bible, though he was not a deeply religious man.

Unlike most boys who were raised on the frontier, Lincoln detested hunting and much preferred spending his spare time engrossed in reading. A few years after his mother died, his family moved to Spencer County, Indiana, and by the time he was 21 the family had moved west into Illinois. Lincoln's first love, Ann Rutledge, died in 1835, and many say that Lincoln never really got over her death. He married Mary Todd when he was 33, and the two had a comfortable marriage until the pressures of public life began to take their toll. She became paranoid, and the death of her son Willie (while Lincoln was president) caused her deep grief.

Lincoln served briefly in the military under the administrations of both Andrew Jackson and Zachary Taylor. His political career began while he was a lawyer in New Salem, Illinois, when he ran unsuccessfully for the state legislature. He was appointed as postmaster of New Salem shortly thereafter by President Jackson. In the election of 1834 Lincoln successfully won a seat in the Illinois legislature and was reelected to three successive terms. He lost his bid for Congress in 1843 but was later successful as he served in Congress from 1843-1847. Then he abandoned his Whig Party in favor of the new Republican Party in 1856 because of his opposition to the extension of slavery. In 1858 he ran for election to the U.S. Senate. His opponent was Stephen Douglas. He lost the election, but he became well known everywhere during the famous series of debates with Stephen Douglas.

ELECTION OF 1860

Lincoln was not the front-runner for the nomination when the Republican convention began. However, by the third ballot, he had surpassed William R. Seward and won the nomination. The nomination for vice president was given to Hannibal Hamlin. The Democratic party finally nominated Stephen A. Douglas for president after much disagreement between Northern and Southern states on the party platform. Their choice for vice president was Benjamin Fitzpatric of Alabama. John C. Breckinridge, vice president under James Buchanan, was chosen as the candidate of the National Democrat Party and John Bell of Tennessee ran on the Constitutional Union Party ticket.

1. While the Democrats were divided regionally with Southerners for Breckinridge and Northerners for Douglas, Republicans were united behind Lincoln. Research the platform of the Republican party and list below its (and Lincoln's) stand on the issues below. Respond on the back of this sheet.

   • secession from the Union

   • slavery in the territories

   • slavery in the South

   • Dred Scott decision

2. Lincoln once said, in one of the famous debates with Stephen Douglas during the Illinois race for the U.S. Senate in 1858, "Moral right—that is the real issue! It is the eternal struggle between these two principles—right and wrong." Yet Lincoln and the Republican Party supported continued slavery in the South during the campaign of 1860. How do you explain this inconsistency? Respond on the back of this sheet.

ELECTION OF 1864

With the nation deeply engrossed in and divided by the Civil War, the Republicans doubted that Lincoln could win reelection. Lincoln himself even conceded that he probably would not win. But Lincoln was still popular with the rank-and-file Republicans, and he was renominated without opposition. Lincoln persuaded his party to nominate Andrew Johnson for vice president rather than Hannibal Hamlin. The Democrats nominated George B. McClellan for president and George H. Pendleton of Ohio for vice president.

3. McClellan was widely regarded as the favorite. Find out how General Sherman's capture of Atlanta helped Lincoln win the election and the significance of the Republican slogan "Don't swap horses in the middle of the stream." Record your response on the back of this sheet.

ANDREW JOHNSON

★ ★

He was the first president to be impeached; however, history has vindicated him as being the victim of some cruel political maneuvering. The plan to remove him from office would have been a black moment in American history had the plan succeeded. Johnson's sudden rise to the presidency when Lincoln was assassinated left him in a position in which it was difficult to please anyone. He was only trying to carry out the lenient plan for reconstruction that had been proposed by President Lincoln. But the Radical Republicans of the North, who wanted to punish the South, combined with the Southern leaders, who had no intention of sharing their power with former slaves, left him in a position in which it was nearly impossible for his administration to accomplish anything.

Andrew Johnson was born in 1808 in a one-story log cottage on the grounds of Casso's Inn in Raleigh, North Carolina. His father was the porter at Casso's Inn as well as being a janitor for the bank, sexton for the church, and town constable. Though poor, his father was a well-respected man. However, he died when young Andrew was only three years old. His mother took in work as a weaver and spinner, and the family lived in extreme poverty throughout Johnson's early years. When he was 14, his mother bound him and his older brother into an indenture agreement as apprentice tailors. After two years, the boys ran away, thus breaking their indenture. They settled in Greeneville, Tennessee, where Johnson opened his own tailor shop at the age of 17.

Johnson did not attend a single day of school in his entire life, but he loved to listen to speeches that had been written by the great orators. He was once given a book of speeches and basically taught himself to read. He would one day become a gifted orator himself. At the age of 18, he married Eliza McCardle, who was only 16 years old. Eliza spent many long hours tutoring Johnson and teaching him to write and figure math.

His political career began with his becoming an alderman in Greeneville, Tennessee. This was followed by his election as the mayor of Greeneville. He was elected to the Tennessee House of Representatives, where he served a term, was then defeated, and was then reelected. Johnson was later elected to the Tennessee state senate before successfully running for Congress in 1843. He was reelected four times. His next political move was election as governor of Tennessee, an office to which he was reelected once. In 1857 he was elected unanimously to the U.S. Senate as a Democrat from Tennessee. While he was a member of the Senate, the Civil War began, with states in the South seceding from the Union. He refused to accept his own state's secession and became the only Southern senator to uphold the Union. He vigorously defended the Lincoln administration and its insistence to "preserve the Union at all costs!"

For his actions, Johnson was regarded as a traitor in the South, and his life was threatened. But in the North, people respected his decision and some regarded his actions as heroic. As a result, Lincoln appointed Johnson as military governor of Tennessee in 1862. His orders were to reestablish federal authority in the state. He did his job well, and Lincoln rewarded him by convincing the Republican Party to choose Johnson over the incumbent Hannibal Hamlin as its vice-presidential candidate for the election of 1864. When Lincoln was assassinated, Vice President Johnson was sworn in as the nation's seventeenth president by Chief Justice Salmon P. Chase.

1. Can you think of any reasons other than Johnson's loyalty to the Union why Lincoln might have wanted Johnson to run as his vice president rather than Hannibal Hamlin, who was Lincoln's vice president during his first term?

   _____

   _____

2. Research the history behind the impeachment of Andrew Johnson. Find out the technicality used to impeach him by those who wanted him out of office.

   _____

   _____

   _____

3. How did the Constitution serve Andrew Johnson well in preventing his being removed from the office of president of the United States?

   _____

   _____

   _____

4. How did the trial of Andrew Johnson save the power of the presidency?

   _____

   _____

   _____

   _____

ULYSSES S. GRANT

★ ★

Courtesy Peter A. Juley & Son

After remaining nameless for a month after birth, he was named Hiram Ulysses Grant. When he was nominated for entry into West Point, he realized that he did not want the initials H.U.G. emblazoned on his equipment, so he signed his name as Ulysses H. Grant. However, the congressman who arranged for his appointment had erroneously called him Ulysses Simpson Grant. Grant went along with the change and his classmates began calling him U.S. or Uncle Sam . . . and eventually just "Sam."

He was born in 1822 in a two-room cabin in Point Pleasant, Ohio, about 25 miles from Cincinnati. His father amassed a small fortune in the tanning industry. Grant was much closer to his mother than his father, and he missed her terribly when he went away to West Point. As a young boy, Grant helped his father clear the land, haul wood, plow fields, and eventually harvest the crops. He avoided his father's tannery whenever possible, because he was squeamish at the sight of blood. He was an extremely honest person, a fact that remains an incongruity considering all the scandal that rocked his administration when he was president.

His early education was mostly at subscription schools, where he was an above-average student. Grant excelled in math and horsemanship, but his sloppy dress and tardiness constantly got him into trouble with those in command. Although military life had no real charm for him, upon graduation he was commissioned a second lieutenant and became involved with the Mexican War. While he publicly opposed the war as immoral, he earned a good service record for his exploits during the war. When the war ended, he moved to the St. Louis area where he tried unsuccessfully to become a farmer and politician.

When the Civil War began, he began working his way up through the ranks and as a military leader became a national hero. His victories earned him the rank of commander of all Union armies, and he accepted the surrender of Lee at Appomattox.

ELECTION OF 1868
When the Republicans convened in 1868, Grant was nominated unanimously on the first ballot. Schuyler Colfax was chosen as the vice-presidential candidate. The Democrats chose Horatio Seymour as their candidate, and Francis P. Blair was the vice-presidential candidate.

1. Grant took no active part in the campaign and made no promises. His campaign theme was simply "Let us have peace." How do you think this campaign slogan might have helped him to win the presidency?

_____

_____

2. The main issue of the campaign was Reconstruction. The Radical Republicans pledged to continue their radical programs that had been enacted over the veto of Andrew Johnson. The Democrats favored more lenient terms. While both parties made their points, Grant won the election for one huge reason. What was this great asset that propelled him to victory?

_____

_____

ELECTION OF 1872

The Republicans renominated Grant in 1872 but chose Henry Wilson as their vice-presidential candidate. Horace Greeley, an influential newspaper owner in New York, was the candidate of the Liberal Republican Party that had grown out of dissatisfaction with the first Grant administration. B. Grates Brown was his vice-presidential choice. The Democrats were in such disarray that they offered no candidate.

3. While Grant was himself an honest man, his administration was tainted with scandal. History ranks Grant near the very bottom as a president. Find out what there was about this man that made him such a poor president.

_____

_____

_____

RUTHERFORD B. HAYES

★ ★

Courtesy Library of Congress, Brady-Handy Collection

He was much more proud of having been a good soldier than he was of his accomplishments as a congressman, the governor of Ohio, and even the president of the United States. Rutherford B. Hayes rose to the rank of major general through his many military exploits. He was wounded on several occasions and even had his horse shot out from under him four times! Hayes was a man of extreme integrity, but he admitted on more than one occasion that he never really wanted the presidency. Nonetheless, he has been placed somewhere near the middle by historians in terms of his effectiveness as president. He always stood firmly behind his principles, and his number-one goal was to "permanently pacify the country by binding the wounds that had torn the nation apart during the Civil War."

Hayes was born in 1822 in the family home in Delaware, Ohio. His father, who was a farmer and merchant who eventually owned his own store, never lived to see his son, as he died 11 weeks before the birth of his son. His mother rented out part of their farm to sustain a livable income. His early education involved several schools in Delaware, Ohio, where he was described as a good student. He graduated from Kenyon College as the class valedictorian, entered Harvard Law School, and was eventually admitted to the Ohio bar.

Hayes neither smoked nor drank. His wife, Lucy Ware Webb, earned the nickname "lemonade Lucy" while she was First Lady, because she refused to allow alcohol to be served in the White House.

When the Civil War broke out, Hayes volunteered and took part in no fewer than 50 engagements! His deeds as a soldier eventually were rewarded with his promotion to the rank of major general, a position he cherished very much.

His political career began in Cincinnati, where he was the city solicitor. From there, he worked his way into a nomination as an Ohio congressman. He won the election and was one of those who voted for the impeachment of Andrew Johnson. Hayes followed his career in Congress with election to the office of governor of Ohio.

ELECTION OF 1876
Hayes was not considered the front-runner when the Republicans convened in Cincinnati in 1876. But the favorite, James C. Blaine, could not win the nomination in the early balloting, and the vote began to shift toward Hayes. He eventually won on the seventh ballot, and his running mate was William Wheeler of New York. The Democrats chose reformer Samuel Tilden, who had brought down the notorious Tweed Ring in New York City. His running mate was William Allen of Ohio.

1. If you research the election of 1876, you will find that Tilden had over 200,000 more popular votes than Hayes. Yet Hayes won the election. How did the Democratically controlled House of Representatives make a tactical blunder by promoting Colorado's admission into the Union, a mistake that cost them the election?

   _____

   _____

2. The Democrats immediately challenged the results of the election on the grounds that three Southern states—Florida, South Carolina, and Louisiana—had been won in the popular vote by Tilden. With these three states, which were in dispute, Hayes would still win the election in the electoral college by a single vote. How did Congress resolve the issue, and how was the eventual outcome a surprise to Rutherford B. Hayes?

   _____

   _____

   _____

3. How did Rutherford B. Hayes eventually quiet the angry Democrats who had cried "fraud" when he won the election?

   _____

   _____

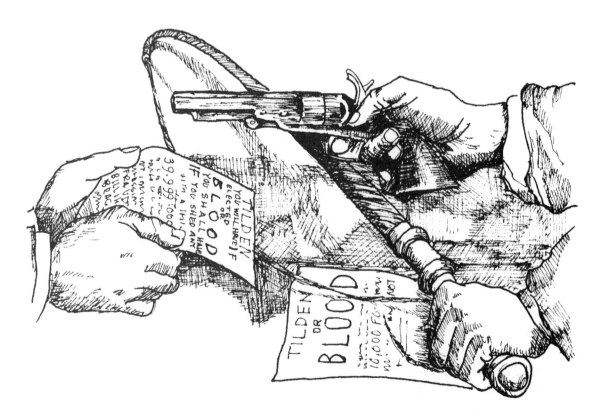

JAMES A. GARFIELD

★★★★★★★★★★★★★★★★★★★★★★★★★

James Garfield "despised a man who blew his own horn." This principle became the guiding force in his life. He was an ambitious man but did little throughout his life to promote his own fortunes. Even in his campaign for the presidency, he left the promotion to others, preferring to remain in the back-ground. Throughout his life, his self-confidence was always fragile.

He was born in 1831 in a log cabin built by his father in Orange, Cuyahoga County, Ohio. His father was a farmer who died when his young son was only 18 months old. Not knowing his father, Garfield's mother soon became the most influential force in his life. He grew up in extreme poverty and, because he was ridiculed by boys who had fathers, he became aggressive and was a good fighter. As a boy, he dreamed of someday living a life at sea. However, his mother convinced him that getting an education was a much more worthwhile pursuit.

Garfield worked his way through the early schools he attended, and eventually he enrolled at Williams College in Massachusetts, where he was a student janitor. When he graduated, he became a teacher. Campus life did not stimulate him, however, and he began to pursue a career in law. He was admitted to the Ohio bar, but he never really practiced law as a career.

As a soldier during the Civil War, Garfield distinguished himself in battle with a number of brilliant performances. Because of his heroics, he was promoted and finally became a major general.

His political career began when he was elected to the Ohio senate in 1859. As a hawk, he welcomed the Civil War and joined the Union army immediately. When the war was over, he was elected to Congress while he was still in uniform. He was among the most radical of Republicans in Congress and was among those who voted for the impeachment of Andrew Johnson. He was implicated in the Credit Mobilier Scandal, though he insisted that he was innocent of any wrongdoing.

ELECTION OF 1880

With the incumbent president Rutherford B. Hayes keeping his pledge not to seek reelection, the front-runner for the Republican nomination was former President Ulysses S. Grant. Also seeking the nomination were John Sherman of Ohio and James G. Blaine of Maine. Garfield supported Sherman and hoped he would win the nomination. As the voting wore on, the delegates began to shift toward Garfield. He eventually garnered enough votes to win the nomination on the thirty-sixth ballot but was stunned by the vote. The vice-presidential nomination went to Chester A. Arthur. The Democrats nominated Winfield S. Hancock for president and William H. English for vice president.

1. Garfield won the popular election by less than 100,000 votes. The vote in the electoral college, however, was a different matter. Garfield won 214 votes, while Hancock won only 155. Both candidates won 19 states. Research the election and explain how Garfield appeared to win the election so handily.

   _____

   _____

2. James A. Garfield was America's president in 1881 only from March 4 to July 2. Find out the circumstances behind his assassination. Who shot President Garfield? What reason did the assassin provide for his deed? Why would Garfield probably not have died if the shooting had taken place today? What was the ultimate fate of Garfield's assassin?

   _____

   _____

   _____

CHESTER A. ARTHUR

★ ★

Courtesy New-York Historical Society

Chester Arthur had never held an elective office until he became vice president. He was known as "Gentleman Boss" and was closely associated with Roscoe Conkling's New York political machine. Arthur had an extensive wardrobe, and he often changed clothes several times a day. He was a man of charm, grace, and polish. When he was elevated to the office of president of the United States, he broke his association with the spoils system and worked very hard for reform. This placed him in a favorable light with many of his former critics and helped to make his job easier.

Arthur was born in 1829 in the parsonage in North Fairfield, Vermont. He was the son of a Baptist minister who moved his family no fewer than 11 times before his retirement. Young Chester was transferred from one school to another in towns throughout Vermont and New York. He entered Union College in 1845 and became a member of Phi Beta Kappa by the time he was a senior. He then studied law at Ballston Spa, New York, and was admitted to the New York bar in 1854.

During the Civil War, Arthur rose through the ranks to become the quartermaster general, a position that placed him in charge of equipping and transporting troops and the munitions of war. He was praised on many occasions for doing his job well. As a result, when the war was over, President Grant appointed him to the lucrative post of collector of the port of New York. This made Arthur responsible for collecting about 75 percent of the nation's duties from ships that entered the port of New York.

During Grant's campaign for reelection to the presidency, Arthur raised contributions for the Republican Party from customhouse employees. His strong alliance with New York party boss Roscoe Conkling earned him the less-than-endearing nickname "a spoilsman's spoilsman."

When Rutherford B. Hayes won the election of 1876, he made it clear that he intended to reform the civil service spoils system of which President Grant had been so much a part. Even though Arthur had collected funds for the Hayes campaign, the new president's reforms extended to the level of Chester Arthur. An investigation was launched, and Hayes found reason to "clean house" in the customhouse. This meant finding a replacement for Arthur. Hayes offered him a job as consul in Paris, but Arthur declined the appointment and resumed his law practice.

1. At the Republican convention in 1880, Chester Arthur was in attendance to serve as a delegate for former President Garfield and as a lieutenant of Stalwart boss Roscoe Conkling. Find out the circumstances under which Arthur actually wound up on the Republican ticket himself as presidential nominee James A. Garfield's vice-presidential candidate.

_____

_____

_____

2. When Chester Arthur became president, he disappointed a spoilsman who came to him seeking a favor by denying the man's request. When the spoilsman reminded Arthur of his former position in the spoils system, Arthur replied, "Since I came here, I've learned that Chester A. Arthur is one man and the president of the United States is another." What do you think he meant by this statement?

_____

_____

3. The name of Chester A. Arthur never appears on any list of America's best presidents. He was not among the most diligent of presidents and admitted that the social aspect was about the only part of the job he really liked. He once confided to a White House clerk that he "never did today what he could put off until tomorrow." Why is this not a good standard for a president to have, and what personal qualities do you think are most important for a person to have who is president of the United States?

_____

_____

GROVER CLEVELAND

★ ★

His massive weight of 250 pounds on a 5 foot, 11-inch frame made him the heaviest president up to that time. His honesty in politics as mayor of Buffalo earned him the nickname of "veto mayor," because he turned down so many appropriation measures proposed by the city council. His hard-work ethic and his driving force toward reform rank him as one of our country's finest presidents.

He was born in 1837 at the Presbyterian manse in Caldwell, New Jersey. His father was a minister; his mother was the daughter of a prosperous publisher. His name came from Reverend Stephen Grover, whom Cleveland's father had succeeded as minister in Caldwell.

As a young boy, Grover Cleveland learned most of his basics from his parents. He wanted to go to college, but his father's death when Grover was only 16 ended those plans and forced him to go to work. He served as editor of *The American Shorthorn Handbook*, a publication owned by a prominent Buffalo stock breeder. He also began studying law on his own at a Buffalo law firm. Cleveland passed the bar exam and was admitted to the New York bar in 1859.

Grover Cleveland was drafted into the military during the Civil War, but he chose to buy a substitute to go in his place. This was a legal option at the time, and Cleveland paid $150 to George Brinske, a Polish immigrant, to serve in his place.

His political career began with his unsuccessful bid to become the state's attorney in Erie County, New York, in 1862. He continued his law practice until he was elected sheriff of Erie County in 1871. His record for instituting reform followed him to Buffalo, where he won an election to become mayor. Again it was his honesty in government that easily won him the election as governor of New York in 1883. As governor, he continued his attack on Tammany Hall and the patronage system that was so commonplace at the time. He promoted much legislation related to the newly created civil service commission, and he also saved over 1.5 million acres around Niagara Falls. His motto became "Public office is a public trust."

ELECTION OF 1884
Cleveland was clearly the front-runner for the presidential nomination when the Democratic convention began, and he easily won the nomination on the second ballot. His running mate was Thomas Hendricks of Indiana. The Republicans nominated James G. Blaine of Maine and chose Arthur Logan as their vice-presidential candidate.

1. The campaign concentrated less on issues and more on the personal morality of the candidates. The Democrats assailed Blaine with their battle cry "Blaine! Blaine! Continental Liar from the State of Maine!" Find out the significance of this slogan and report your answer in the space below.

   _____

   _____

2. The Republicans threw their own darts at Cleveland with the campaign chant "Ma, Ma, Where's my Pa? Gone to the White House, ha, ha, ha!" Find out the significance of this slogan meant to degrade Grover Cleveland and record your answer below.

   _____

   _____

   _____

3. Everyone knew the election would be very close. New York was the crucial state both candidates felt they needed to win the election. Find out how Blaine and the Republican Party alienated the Irish Catholics of New York, causing the Republicans to lose the state and, hence, the election.

   _____

   _____

   _____

   _____

BENJAMIN HARRISON

★ ★

Benjamin Harrison's grandfather, William Henry Harrison, had been America's ninth president. Benjamin's personality lacked charisma, and he was stiff and formal with people. He was sometimes called the "human iceberg," but he was a man of honesty and integrity, and he was also an excellent orator.

Benjamin Harrison was born in 1833 in the home of his famous grandfather in North Bend, Ohio. His father, John Scott Harrison, has been the only man to be both the son of a president and the father of another. Harrison's childhood was spent much like that of any other young farm boy. Young Benjamin truly enjoyed doing his chores, and he loved the great outdoors. He decided at an early age that he wanted to become either a minister or a lawyer.

His early education came mostly from tutors who were at his home, but he also spent many long hours reading in his grandfather's huge library. He eventually enrolled at Miami University in Ohio, where he graduated near the top of his class. By then he had decided to pursue a career in law, and he became a lawyer in 1854.

Harrison served in the military during the Civil War. Although he performed admirably on the battlefield, he had no real taste for military life. In 1876 he ran unsuccessfully for governor of Indiana. Soon after that the Indiana state legislature elected him to serve in the U.S. Senate. He tried to win the seat for a second term, but his bid for reelection fell short. Soon after that defeat, he announced that he would be running for president.

ELECTION OF 1888

When the Republicans gathered for their national convention in Chicago, James G. Blaine was the front-runner, but he quickly withdrew his name from nomination because he felt that only a united Republican effort would have any chance at all of upsetting the incumbent Grover Cleveland. Harrison quietly gained support as the balloting wore on. Finally, by the seventh ballot, he had taken the lead, and by the eighth ballot he had enough votes to win the nomination. The vice-presidential nomination went to Levi P. Morton. The Democrats unanimously chose President Cleveland and nominated Allen G. Thurman as their choice for vice president.

Courtesy Benjamin H. Walker

1. The campaign was among the most decent in history. There was no name-calling, no mudslinging, and neither candidate even personally hit the campaign trail. Yet the election was extremely close. In fact, Cleveland actually won the popular vote. Research the results of the election of 1888 and record below how many more popular votes Cleveland had than Harrison.

   _____

   _____

2. Ironically, Cleveland lost the election because he failed to carry his home state of New York. Research this strange circumstance and explain below how he lost New York . . . and ultimately the election. Support your answer with electoral college results.

   _____

   _____

   _____

3. One of the criticisms lodged against Harrison concerned his handshake, which many compared to "a wilted petunia." First, what is meant by this analogy? Next, why is it especially important for a president (and actually anyone else seeking success) to have a firm handshake?

   _____

   _____

   _____

GROVER CLEVELAND

★ ★

When Grover Cleveland was 27 years old, he met his future wife shortly after she was born. Frances Folsom was the daughter of Oscar Folsom, a close friend of Cleveland. When her father died without a will, the court appointed Cleveland as the administrator of Folsom's estate. Cleveland remained in close contact with Frances Folsom and doted over her like a father. When she was in college, his feelings began to take a more romantic turn.

When Folsom graduated from college, Cleveland proposed marriage to her by letter. Cleveland was 49 years old and president of the United States at the time. Folsom was just 21 years old. The two did not announce their engagement until just five days before the wedding. Their wedding was and remains today the only occasion when a president was actually married in the White House.

Since she was the youngest First Lady ever, Mrs. Cleveland was the subject of much attention by the Washington press. Cleveland's first term in office met with general approval from the public. The civil reformers liked what he was doing, and businessmen praised his sound money practices. But then he lost the close election of 1888 to Benjamin Harrison. After that election, as the Clevelands were preparing to leave the White House, Cleveland's young wife told the White House staff that they would be back in four years—and she was right!

ELECTION OF 1892
Even though Cleveland had lost the election of 1888, he was clearly the front-runner for the Democratic nomination in 1892. However, he still faced a certain amount of opposition from Tammany men, who frequently vented their hostilities toward Cleveland on the convention floor. Cleveland did survive to narrowly win the nomination on the first ballot. Adlai E. Stevenson of Illinois was nominated as the Democratic vice-presidential candidate. The Republicans nominated incumbent President Benjamin Harrison as their presidential candidate and chose Whitelaw Reid as their vice-presidential nominee.

1. The campaign of 1892 was rather lackluster, with the tariff issue being the dominant factor. Both candidates stopped campaigning when First Lady Caroline Harrison suddenly died. There was a third-party candidate in this election who actually won four western states. Research the results of this election and find out his name, the name of his party, the four states he won, and the reason for his popularity in the West.

_____

_____

_____

2. While Cleveland's first term in the White House had gone rather smoothly, his second term was anything but smooth! The Panic of 1893 touched off a widespread, long-lasting depression. Unemployment, labor unrest, and the rise of Populism all contributed to Cleveland's problems. When he left the White House after his term expired, he was one of the most unpopular men in the country. Yet history has been kind to Grover Cleveland, and his name always rises to the top third whenever there is a poll that evaluates American presidents. Read from other sources about this unique man and decide whether or not you think he would be a good president in today's world.

_____

_____

_____

3. Why do you think Cleveland decided to run for president again after being defeated in the election of 1888?

_____

_____

_____

1892

WILLIAM MCKINLEY

★ ★ ★ ★ ★ ★ ★ ★ ★ ★ ★ ★ ★ ★ ★ ★ ★ ★ ★ ★

He was the only clean-shaven president between Andrew Johnson and Woodrow Wilson. William McKinley stood only 5 feet 7 inches tall, but he weighed nearly 200 pounds. He was a handsome man with a strong, clear voice and a friendly, even temper that made him well-liked by most people he encountered. McKinley was even described as "beloved" by one historian, and his years in the White House rank him near the middle in effectiveness as a president. However, he was the third American president to be felled by an assassin's bullet, when a deranged, unemployed Polish mill worker fired the fatal shots on September 5, 1901.

McKinley was born in 1843 in a small house in Niles, Ohio. His father was a successful pig iron manufacturer; his mother was a deeply religious woman who had a very close relationship with her son. Young William attended public schools in Niles, Ohio, where his favorite subject was speech. He entered Allegheny College in Pennsylvania but was forced to drop out when the Depression of 1857 depleted the family finances. McKinley taught school for awhile; then he studied law and was eventually admitted to the Ohio bar in 1867.

McKinley was cited on a number of occasions for his heroic deeds during the Civil War. Following the war, McKinley developed his law practice and began to rise through the ranks of the Republican party. He was first elected Stark County prosecutor and then was elected to Congress, representing the Eighteenth District in the state of Ohio. He earned his national reputation in the House of Representatives as the champion of protectionism through a high tariff. While this proved unpopular with many voters, he was still popular within the ranks of his own party. He was elected governor of Ohio in 1892 and reelected two years later.

ELECTION OF 1896

When the Republicans convened in 1896, McKinley was the front-runner for the nomination. He was nominated on the first ballot, and Garret A. Hobart was the Republican choice for vice president. The Democrats chose William Jennings Bryan as their nominee for president and Arthur Sewall of Maine for vice president. However, the Eastern Democrats were unable to accept the Democratic platform, which included a call for the free coinage of silver. So they chose a candidate of their own, John M. Palmer of Illinois, and called themselves the National, or Gold Democrats.

1. Bryan, the Democratic candidate, launched a vigorous, all-out campaign, and he traveled by rail over 18,000 miles in just three months. McKinley, on the other hand, ventured no further than the front porch of his house to speak to delegations that came to him. Nonetheless, McKinley had literally hundreds of workers campaigning for him all over the nation. The amount of money collected by the Republicans for the campaign totaled nearly five times as much as the Democrats had available for campaign expenditures. McKinley won the election. How do you think McKinley's campaign tactics would fly if he were campaigning for president today?

   _____

   _____

ELECTION OF 1900

McKinley's renomination was a sure bet when the Republicans gathered in Philadelphia in June of 1900. However, their choice for vice president, Theodore Roosevelt, was reluctant to give up the governorship of New York. In the end he was convinced that he would serve his country best by accepting the nomination. The Democrats once again chose William Jennings Bryan and nominated Adlai E. Stevenson of Illinois for vice president.

2. With additional gold discovered in Alaska and elsewhere, the currency issue was not the main concern in the election of 1900. The big issue was imperialism. The Spanish-American War had been regarded by many Americans as unnecessary and a reason to take command of lands in far distant places. The Republicans countered with Theodore Roosevelt's call for "Four More Years of the Full Dinner Pail." Find out the meaning of this Republican campaign slogan that helped them to capture the White House one more time.

   _____

   _____

   _____

3. While the aggression of Spain in blowing up the U.S. battleship *Maine* ultimately led to the Spanish-American War, America was labeled an imperialist around the world for the results of the Paris Peace Treaty of 1898. Find out the terms of that treaty and list the reasons for some Americans being unhappy with McKinley's aggression.

   _____

   _____

   _____

   _____

   _____

THEODORE ROOSEVELT

★★★★★★★★★★★★★★★★★★★★★★★★★

The toy teddy bear was named for Theodore Roosevelt after a cartoon depicted him sparing the life of a bear cub while hunting. He was spindly and asthmatic as a boy, but he built himself up through vigorous exercise into a brawny man with a barrel chest and energy to burn. He was no doubt the most energetic of our presidents. As the leader of the Rough Riders, he became legendary, and his foreign policy approach of "speak softly and carry a big stick" was very popular among Americans.

Theodore Roosevelt was born in 1858 at the family brownstone on East 20th Street in New York City. His father, Theodore Roosevelt, Sr., was "the best man I ever knew," according to the man who became president when William McKinley was assassinated. His mother had been a fashionable Southern belle before she met and married Theodore's father.

Because he was a sickly youth, he was unable to attend public schools, so most of his fundamental education came from his maternal aunt, Annie Bulloch. During his childhood he became determined to overcome his illnesses and improve his scrawny physique. He studied in Germany for a time and later returned to the United States and enrolled at Harvard. His early love for the great outdoors made him want to become a naturalist, but he changed his mind and decided to attend law school. However, he dropped out of Columbia Law School to run for the state assembly.

His bravery and heroism during the Spanish-American War made him an extremely popular personality with the American public. His political career had begun years earlier when he was elected to the New York state assembly. He was then appointed to the U.S. Civil Service Commission by President Benjamin Harrison. He followed this by serving as president of the New York City Police Board. President McKinley appointed him assistant secretary of the navy. In 1898 he won election as the governor of New York. When he was asked to run as McKinley's vice president, he refused at first because he did not want to give up the governorship of New York. Friends and political allies convinced him to run and, when McKinley died from an assassin's bullet, Roosevelt was elevated to the office of president of the United States.

1. Perhaps Roosevelt understood the power of good publicity better than any president who had preceded him. Even though he was president a century ago, he had the right idea. Why is it so important for the president of the United States to have a good relationship and image with the press?

_____

_____

ELECTION OF 1904

Roosevelt's renomination was assured when the Republicans convened in June of 1904. In fact, he was nominated unanimously, carrying all 994 votes. Charles W. Fairbanks of Indiana was chosen as the vice-presidential candidate. The Democrats nominated Alton B. Parker for president and Henry G. Davis as their vice-presidential candidate.

2. Since both parties had somewhat similar platforms, the campaign turned into a battle of personalities. And here the flamboyant and very popular Roosevelt was the winner without a contest over the colorless and sober style and personality of Parker. Neither candidate launched an aggressive campaign. Research the results of the election. What was Roosevelt's margin of victory? Look at the demographics of this election and report below those sections of the country that carried Roosevelt to victory.

_____

_____

3. Though he loved war, Roosevelt kept the United States out of war during his seven and one-half years as president. His accomplishments rank him among America's finest presidents. He has also been honored by representation on Mt. Rushmore. Research the Roosevelt years and report below why you think he has such a lofty rank among American presidents.

_____

_____

_____

WILLIAM HOWARD TAFT

★★★★★★★★★★★★★★★★★★★★★★★★★★★★

William Howard Taft was the largest of our presidents, weighing nearly 340 pounds. In fact, he once got stuck in the White House bathtub and had to have an oversized model brought in for his own use. He was cheerful and popular among people, but he had few close friends. He was also terrible at remembering names and often made tactless remarks that offended others. "Big Bill" was sometimes even accused of being lazy and was caught on more than one occasion dozing off during cabinet meetings, White House dinners, and news conferences. But his accomplishments during his four years of office were at least respectable and historians rank him right near the middle in terms of an effective administration.

Taft was born in 1857 in his parents' home in Cincinnati, Ohio. His father was a lawyer, a cabinet officer, and a diplomat, serving in many official public capacities. His mother was the daughter of a Boston merchant, a strong-willed woman who discouraged her son from seeking the presidency.

Taft grew up in Cincinnati, enjoying a fun-filled childhood that included many friends who often referred to him as "Big Lub." He attended public schools in Cincinnati in the Mount Auburn section of the city, where he was an excellent student. He enrolled at Yale University and graduated four years later as salutatorian of the class. After that came Cincinnati Law School and admission to the Ohio bar in 1880.

Taft's political career began as assistant prosecutor of Hamilton County, Ohio. He then became assistant solicitor of Hamilton County, U.S. solicitor general, and judge of the Sixth U.S. Circuit Court. President McKinley appointed him to the post of governor-general, a position in which he was assigned to establish civil government in the newly acquired Philippines. His immense success in this assignment led President Roosevelt to appoint him secretary of war. Roosevelt also nominated him to the Supreme Court, but Taft reluctantly declined because he still had some "unfinished business in the War Department." By this time he was recognized as the leading candidate for the Republican nomination for president.

ELECTION OF 1908

William Howard Taft had always wanted to serve on the Supreme Court, but he did say that he would accept a draft as the nominee for president if that was the will of his Republican party. Incumbent President Theodore Roosevelt felt that he had served two terms (the remaining three and one-half years of McKinley's term plus his own election in

1904), so he declined to seek a third term. Roosevelt's choice as his successor was William Howard Taft, who won the nomination on the first ballot. The vice-presidential nominee was James S. Sherman of New York. The Democratic opponents were William Jennings Bryan for president and John W. Kern of Indiana for vice president.

1. Both candidates banked on ties with former President Theodore Roosevelt to help carry them through. Taft was the hand-picked choice of Roosevelt as his successor, and Bryan claimed that Roosevelt had largely co-opted the Democratic platform and that he and not Taft would carry on Roosevelt's war against large trusts and those who would rob our nation of its natural resources. But William Jennings Bryan made a big mistake during the campaign when he took a stand regarding the nation's railroads. Find out what his position was and how it was received by the American voting public.

   _____

   _____

2. During the Taft administration, the term *Dollar Diplomacy* became commonplace in the language of American citizens. Find out the meaning of this term and how it was significant to the William Howard Taft years in the White House.

   _____

   _____

   _____

3. While Theodore Roosevelt and William Howard Taft had been good friends and political allies (with Taft being chosen by Roosevelt as his hand-picked successor), the two became political enemies. Find out the circumstances that surrounded this feud and record your response below.

   _____

   _____

   _____

WOODROW WILSON

★ ★

Woodrow Wilson was the devout son of a Presbyterian minister who grew up with a belief in religious destiny—his own. When he ran for president, he felt that it was God's will that he would win. He lacked confidence in his own appearance and often said the following to himself: "For beauty I am not a star. There are others more handsome by far. But my face I don't mind it. For I am behind it. It's the people in front that I jar." This self-deprecatory limerick helped Wilson to forge on confidently despite his somewhat homely appearance.

He was born in 1856 in the Presbyterian manse in Staunton, Virginia. His father was a staunch supporter of the South during the Civil War. Woodrow Wilson was deeply devoted to his mother, who emigrated to Ohio from England when she was four years old. Wilson's childhood was filled with impressions of the Civil War and the painful humiliation of Reconstruction. His early education came from his parents, and he was nine years old before he could read! His frail health often undermined his attempts at school, but he entered Davidson College in 1873. He was forced to drop out at the end of his freshman year because of his poor health. He later enrolled at the College of New Jersey (later Princeton) where he excelled. On graduation, he entered the University of Virginia Law School but again dropped out for health reasons. He had decided early in life that he wanted to pursue a career in politics.

His career began as a teacher at Bryn Mawr College, where he taught political economy and public law. In 1902 he was named president of Princeton University. In 1911 he was elected governor of New Jersey. He immediately declared war on the big machine bosses, pledging to "lance them like warts from body parts." Under his leadership, several laws were passed to control the big trusts. However, some were repealed after he left office.

ELECTION OF 1912
While Wilson aggressively sought the Democratic nomination for president in 1912, the road to success was difficult. As the convention wore on, he eventually gained the endorsement of William Jennings Bryan and won the nomination on the forty-sixth ballot. His vice-presidential running mate was Thomas R. Marshall of Indiana. The Republicans endorsed incumbent William Howard Taft, but the nomination did not come easily. Former President Theodore Roosevelt, who had chosen Taft to succeed him, decided to run again and launched an aggressive campaign that left the Republican convention in total confusion. The result was Taft's nomination, but Roosevelt became a strong candidate on his own through his Bull Moose Party nomination.

1. Since the Republicans were divided between Taft and Roosevelt, Wilson was virtually assured of election. But the campaign was nonetheless a spirited event. A week before the election, Wilson was listed as a 6:1 odds favorite to win the election. His election was not nearly so overwhelming. Research the results of this election and decide why you think Wilson won.

_____

_____

_____

_____

ELECTION OF 1916

When the Democrats convened in St. Louis in June of 1916, Wilson was the clear-cut favorite for renomination. Vice President Marshall was also renominated. The Republicans chose Charles Evans Hughes of New York. Their choice for vice president was Charles W. Fairbanks.

2. The campaign cry of the Democratic Party was "He kept us out of war!" The Republicans countered with Wilson's failure to assert American neutral rights as World War I waged on. The election promised to be a close one, with most of the media predicting a very close election. It was indeed that! Research the final numbers in the election of 1916 and decide why you think Wilson won.

_____

_____

_____

_____

3. Research one of the following and record your answer on the back of this sheet.

   a. Wilson has been evaluated as "America's fourth greatest president." Research his accomplishments and decide why you think he ranks as one of America's best presidents.

   b. Even though Wilson himself finally asked Congress to declare war against Germany, he was awarded the Nobel Peace Prize in 1919. Find out what Wilson did to become deserving of this high honor.

   c. Once the Treaty of Versailles had been signed, Wilson directed his energy toward creating the League of Nations. Why did the United States not join the League?

WARREN G. HARDING

★ ★

Courtesy Library of Congress

Warren G. Harding has the dubious distinction of being labeled by those who rank the accomplishments of our presidents "Our Nation's Worst President." Although he was an honest man himself, some of the men he appointed to high places were nothing more than crooks. He developed a reputation for playing poker with his cronies in the White House as well as providing a free flow of liquor there during Prohibition. In addition, he had a widely known reputation for being unfaithful to his wife. Perhaps the final blow to his reputation was his willingness to admit that he had neither the intelligence nor the experience to satisfactorily handle the job of being America's president. In the end, distress from the pressure placed on him for his errors led to his untimely death while on a vacation and speech-making tour in San Francisco.

Harding was born in 1865 in the family farmhouse in Corsica, Ohio. His father was a doctor, as was his mother. His childhood was a pleasant one, filled with the virtues of village life. He delighted in his farm chores and spent many hours in delightful play with his friends. Most of his early education came from his mother, who spent hours and hours teaching him the basics. When he was 15, he entered Ohio Central College where he eventually graduated. He loved to play cards, and he developed an early reputation for gambling. Harding also enjoyed playing golf and considered it an important part of his life even when he was president.

Upon graduation from college, Harding taught school for one year outside Marion, Ohio. At the end of the term, he decided it was not the life for him, and he began studying law. He eventually bought a local newspaper with two other partners. The paper was a financial success, and Harding began to prosper. He was elected to the Ohio senate in 1899, then won a second term, and later became the majority floor leader. In 1903 Harding was elected lieutenant governor of Ohio under Governor Myron T. Herrick. He later won election to the U.S. Senate. While in the Senate, Harding developed a reputation for poor attendance and for not doing the proper research that would have made him better informed.

ELECTION OF 1920
Harding's Republican campaign manager predicted that Harding would not win the nomination on the first ballot, nor the second ballot, nor even the third. But Daugherty declared that Harding would indeed win the nomination as the "dark-horse" candidate. That he did on the tenth ballot, and his running mate became Governor Calvin Coolidge of Massachusetts. The Democrats chose James M. Cox of Ohio to run for president and Franklin D. Roosevelt as their vice president.

1. The election itself was a referendum on the Wilson administration and the League of Nations. While Harding conducted nothing more than a front-porch campaign, the Democrats sent Cox on a 22,000-mile train journey to campaign literally everywhere he could possibly go. But in the end, Harding won the election handily. America's participation (or lack of it) in the League of Nations was one of the key issues of the campaign. Find out the stand each of the candidates took on the issue and explain your answer in the space below.

   _____

   _____

   _____

2. Once in the White House, Harding actually did make some wise choices to fill the empty seats of his new cabinet. Charles Evans Hughes, Andrew Mellon, and Herbert Hoover were among his good choices. But Harding made enough bad choices that his reputation became sullied along the way as a man of few principles and very poor judgment. Find out some of his bad choices and record their government positions in the space below.

   _____

   _____

   _____

3. Research one of the following and record your findings on the back of this sheet.
   a. Find out the scandal behind the Teapot Dome Affair and explain.
   b. How did Harding ensure the ultimate failure of the League of Nations?

CALVIN COOLIDGE

★ ★

Courtesy Library of Congress

When Calvin Coolidge became president after Harding's death, the country "wanted nothing done," as one White House aid suggested, ". . . and he done it." He did less work and made fewer decisions than perhaps any other president of the United States. One person who was close to him when he was president said of Coolidge, "He slept more and did less than any president ever!" He had a reputation for sleeping nine hours at night and taking a two-hour nap every day, giving him 11 hours of sleep virtually every day. Coolidge was also a man of few words with this philosophy: "If you don't say anything, you can't be called on to repeat it!" His close-mouthed stay in the White House became his hallmark, and his record was almost a blank. But many of the few statements he did make became historically famous. His wit and frugal way of living made him a popular figure with the American public. When he died, a writer from the *New Yorker* asked the question, "How can they tell?"

John Calvin Coolidge was born in 1872 in the family home adjoining the Coolidge general store in Plymouth, Vermont. His father was a successful farmer, storekeeper, and eventually public servant, serving in the Vermont state house of representatives, later the Vermont state senate, and finally as a justice of the peace. Coolidge inherited his delicate features and size from his mother, who died of tuberculosis when Calvin was only 12 years old.

His early education came from public schools in Plymouth, Vermont. Coolidge, who was a loner, seemed quite content with doing his chores at home on the farm after each school day had ended. He then took preparatory exams to gain entrance to Amhurst College, but he failed the first time. He then went to St. Johnsbury, where he took enough instruction to gain entrance into Amhurst. He began to apply himself and eventually graduated from Amhurst. After graduation, he began to pursue a career in the field of law, and he gained admission to the bar in 1897.

His political career began with election to local offices in the Northampton, Massachusetts, area. Coolidge then won two consecutive terms in the Massachusetts state legislature. This was followed with two terms as mayor of Northampton. In 1912 he won election to the Massachusetts state senate, where he served four consecutive terms. He then became lieutenant governor of Massachusetts and followed that with election as governor of Massachusetts. He was a "favorite son" candidate in the Republican convention of 1920, but in reality he was not on the list of "possible" candidates. He was not a favorite for the vice-presidential nomination either, but he suddenly became a factor and actually won on the first ballot.

He was vacationing in Vermont at his father's home when word came that President Warren G. Harding had died of an apparent heart attack. As a justice of the peace, Coolidge's father was able to administer the presidential oath of office to Calvin in the middle of the night on August 3, 1923. When the swearing in was over, Calvin went back to bed for the rest of the night. He then served out the remainder of Harding's term of office.

ELECTION OF 1924

At the Republican convention in 1924, Coolidge was the overwhelming favorite, winning easily on the first ballot. Charles G. Dawes of Illinois was chosen as the vice-presidential candidate. The Democrats finally chose John W. Davis as their dark-horse candidate after the longest stalemate in political convention history, in which they voted 100 times without a winner! Their vice-presidential choice was Charles W. Bryan, brother of William Jennings Bryan.

1. With the country prosperous, the nation at peace, and the integrity of the executive branch restored in the wake of Harding's disastrous administration, the Republican slogan became, "Keep Cool with Coolidge!" However, the term *cool* did not mean what it came to mean years later or what it means today. Do a little research and find out what the Republicans meant by their slogan.

   _____

   _____

   _____

2. His performance as president ranked him near the bottom of the barrel, mainly because he did not do much as president. He remained fairly noncommital on almost every issue presented to him. While this policy might have been popular at the time (it must have been because he won the 1924 election handily), why would this lack of commitment to issues be unacceptable today?

   _____

   _____

1924

HERBERT HOOVER

★ ★

Courtesy Library of Congress

He had a reputation for unusual intelligence, high energy, extreme efficiency, and humanitarian concern. He was a wealthy mining engineer who turned to public service during World War I and gained a worldwide reputation when he served as director of Woodrow Wilson's food administration. He was sought after by both parties as a "great candidate" for president. Young Franklin D. Roosevelt proclaimed that "there couldn't be a better one!" His election to the presidency in 1928 was the only elected office he ever held. A few months after his election, the nation went into its worst financial tailspin in history, and Herbert Hoover unfortunately got the blame for much of it. While he took more action than any previous president had taken during a depression, he simply could not get on top of the situation. Historians rank him "below average" in his performance as president.

He was born in 1874 in a small cottage in West Branch, Iowa. At the age of two, he developed a severe case of croup and his parents gave him up for dead. Fortunately, his uncle, Dr. John Minthorn, arrived in time to revive him. His father was a blacksmith, farm equipment salesman, and town councilman who died of heart trouble when Herbert was only six years old. Hoover's mother tried to keep the family going by taking in sewing. She became a Quaker minister and developed pneumonia after speaking at a Friends meeting on a cold winter evening. She died shortly thereafter, and Hoover became an orphan at the age of nine. From that point he was raised by his Uncle John, the nonpacifist Quaker who had earlier saved his life.

Hoover's early education was in the West Branch Free School, but his Uncle John took him to Oregon when his parents died. He attended schools there and eventually gained entrance into Stanford University. He loved engineering and eventually graduated from Stanford with a degree in geology. Hoover's first major job as an engineer took him to Coolgardie, Australia, where he evaluated mines prior to purchase. He later transferred to China, where he served as China's mining engineer. He then returned to Australia and developed the lucrative zinc mining industry. It was later in Burma that he made much of his fortune, with his development of the Bawdwin silver mine. He then formed his own engineering firm and expanded his wealth through mining developments all over the world.

During World War I he served as the head of the American Relief Committee that helped get food and supplies to 120,000 Americans stranded in Europe. He then became America's food administrator and served on the war trade council. He was Wilson's economic advisor at the Treaty of Versailles. Hoover was chosen as secretary of commerce by President Harding and remained in the position under the Coolidge administration.

ELECTION OF 1928

When the Republicans convened in 1928, President Coolidge addressed the convention with, "I do not choose to run." As a result, Hoover became the obvious choice, and he won on the first ballot. His running mate was Charles Curtis. The Democrats nominated Alfred E. Smith for president and Senator Joseph T. Robinson for vice president.

1. Because Alfred E. Smith was the first Catholic to run for president on a major party ticket, religion became a big issue. There were rumors that a Catholic president would be little more than a "tool of the Pope." Herbert Hoover's campaign was above this type of talk, and he concentrated on more positive issues. A popular Republican campaign slogan was "a chicken in every pot and a car in every garage." What did the tone of this campaign promise mean?

   _____

   _____

2. Another Republican campaign slogan was "Let's Keep What We've Got!" This slogan warned Americans against tampering with the economic success of the times. The Democrats countered with Smith's campaign theme "The Sidewalks of New York," which heralded the humble beginnings of Smith, who grew up amid poverty on the Lower East Side. Smith was quick-witted and colorful and impressive before people. Hoover was lackluster at best, but the election was not even close! Find out why Hoover won so handily.

   _____

   _____

   _____

3. Hoover was inaugurated on March 4, 1929. On October 29, the stock market crashed, sending America into its deepest and most severe depression ever. Find out what caused the market to crash. Do you think Hoover should have been blamed?

   _____

   _____

   _____

   _____

FRANKLIN DELANO ROOSEVELT

★ ★

Courtesy Library of Congress

In 1940 he brushed aside the unwritten law that allowed presidents to serve no more than two terms in office by running for a third term. In 1944 he won election to the White House for a fourth time. "It may be unorthodox," he said, "but it's doing the country good." While some Americans had serious doubts about his ability to handle the presidency, he proved them wrong by displaying remarkable gifts for leadership in a time of true crisis. His New Deal led the nation out of its worst financial condition ever with a program that bordered on a mix of capitalism, socialism, perhaps even a touch of communism. He was the recipient of passionate adoration and blind hatred. But in the end the United States was a better country because he had been its president. Historians are pretty much in agreement that he belongs behind only Lincoln and Washington in the rank of America's greatest presidents.

He was born in 1882, in the family home in Hyde Park, New York. The name Delano was given him to honor his great-uncle Franklin Hughes Delano. His father was a lawyer and financier who lived much of his life as a wealthy country squire at Hyde Park. He was a founder and director of the Consolidated Coal Company, president of the Southern Railway Security Company, and a director of the Delaware and Hudson Railroad. His mother was the daughter of a merchant who had made his fortune in trade with China. Roosevelt had a half brother by his father's first marriage. He was his mother's only child.

Young Franklin grew up in the protective atmosphere of Hyde Park and the Roosevelt summer place on Campobello Island. His early education came from a series of private tutors. He attended a public school in Germany for a short time while traveling abroad with his parents. In 1896 he entered Groton, where he was considered an above-average student. Upon graduation, he entered Harvard, where his most cherished accomplishment was serving as editor-in-chief of the Harvard *Crimson*. He even stayed an extra year at Harvard to work on the paper. During that time he took several graduate courses but did not earn a master's degree. He then entered Columbia Law School, but he never graduated from law school, as he dropped out of school after passing the bar exam.

His joys in life included swimming, watching birds, sailing, collecting stamps, fishing, and watching motion pictures. One day when he was 21, he helped some local residents on Campobello Island fight a forest fire. When the fire was out, he took a cold dip in the Bay of Fundy. He then jogged the mile back to his home, where, still in his wet swimming trunks, he went through his mail. That night he went to bed with the chills. Two days later he could not move his legs. He was soon diagnosed as a victim of poliomyelitis. Through a vigorous exercise program, Roosevelt was able to stand with braces and walk briefly with crutches.

When he was 23, he married Eleanor Roosevelt, his fifth cousin once removed. She was given in marriage by her uncle, then-President Theodore Roosevelt. Eleanor would later become one of America's best-known and well-loved women. Roosevelt's political career began with his election to the New York state senate. After serving two terms, he was appointed by President Woodrow Wilson as assistant secretary of the navy. He ran unsuccessfully for the Democratic nomination for the U.S. Senate in 1914. During World War I, he directed the mining of waters between Scotland and Norway. He accepted the Democratic vice-presidential nomination on the ticket of James M. Cox in 1920, and he campaigned vigorously for Alfred E. Smith during his unsuccessful campaigns in both 1924 and 1928. In 1928 Roosevelt was elected governor of New York and won reelection in 1930.

ELECTION OF 1932

When the Democrats convened in Chicago in 1932, Roosevelt was the front-runner for the nomination. Alfred E. Smith was a contender, but Roosevelt was nominated on the fourth ballot. His running mate was John Nance Garner of Texas. The Republicans chose President Herbert Hoover and also renominated Vice President Charles Curtis.

1. The Great Depression was of course the main issue that dominated the campaigns of the 1932 election. Beneath the surface of the election were the doubts that an invalid would be able to handle the rigors of the presidency. To combat this, Roosevelt launched a vigorous campaign, delivering nearly 60 speeches around the nation. Research Hoover's campaign. How did he handle the pressure of being an incumbent president thrust into the role of underdog because of the hostilities he faced due to the Depression? What was Roosevelt's promise of a New Deal?

   _____

   _____

   _____

   _____

   _____

   _____

2. The Republicans landed on the campaign slogan "Play Safe with Hoover," while the Democrats used as their campaign song "Happy Days Are Here Again." In the end, the people chose Roosevelt. Research the results of the election. Was it a close election, or did Roosevelt win by a landslide? Record your findings in the space below.

   _____

   _____

   _____

ELECTION OF 1936

When the Democrats convened in Philadelphia in 1936, it was obvious that President Roosevelt was the man they wanted to run for president. They also chose Vice President John Nance Garner for vice president. The Republicans chose Alf M. Landon as their candidate for president and Frank Knox of Illinois as their vice-presidential candidate.

3. While Landon approved of the overall goals of Roosevelt's New Deal, he disapproved of the methods Roosevelt used. Find out what it was that he did not like about the Roosevelt campaign policy and what he proposed to do to eliminate the problem.

_____

_____

_____

_____

4. The American people overwhelmingly reelected President Roosevelt in 1936 by a vote of 523 to 8 in the electoral college. In fact, Landon suffered the worst defeat in modern-day history, winning only two states. Which two states did he win?

_____

ELECTION OF 1940

While the Democrats were uncertain whether or not Roosevelt would seek an unprecedented third term, he decided to break tradition because he liked being president and because his presidency had ". . . done the country good." With that, he was promptly renominated for a third term. Roosevelt dumped Vice President Garner and chose Henry A. Wallace of Iowa as his running mate. The Republicans chose Wendall Wilkie as their man for president and Charles McNary of Oregon for vice president.

5. The war in Europe and Roosevelt's running for a third term were the two big issues of the campaign. Wilkie launched a major attack on Roosevelt's breaking the unwritten rule of serving only two terms that had been established by George Washington and honored by all presidents before Roosevelt. What is your opinion on the matter? Are two terms enough? Or should a president be allowed to serve as many terms as the American public chooses?

_____

_____

_____

_____

_____

_____

6. Which candidate won the farm vote? Which candidate won the villages, towns, and small cities? Which candidate won all cities in the entire country with populations exceeding 400,000 except Cincinnati? Does this help to explain why Roosevelt won the election so handily?

_____

_____

_____

ELECTION OF 1944

At the 1944 Democratic convention, Roosevelt was chosen on the first ballot. Because of his failing health, many delegates felt that choosing the vice-presidential candidate would in effect be choosing the next president. Therefore, they forced Roosevelt to abandon Vice President Wallace and choose someone else. A bitter fight erupted and the eventual winner of the vice-presidential nomination was Harry Truman of Missouri. The Republicans chose Thomas Dewey of New York as their candidate for president and John W. Bricker of Ohio as their vice-presidential candidate.

7. While Dewey declined to make an issue of America's involvement in World War II, he did dwell on Roosevelt's age and failing health. The Democrats launched their campaign on the charge, "Don't Change Horses in Midstream!" The voters once again responded to Roosevelt's appeal and elected him as their president. Research the election and find out the results. How did Roosevelt's victory compare with his other elections as president? Was it close? Was it a landslide? Report your findings in the space below.

_____

_____

_____

HARRY S TRUMAN

★ ★

Courtesy Harry S Truman Library of Congress

FDR had been president of the United States for so long that it was difficult for the American people and the press to think of Harry Truman as their president. In fact, it took Truman himself awhile to get used to the notion that he was indeed the president. He had loved serving in the U.S. Senate, and he was reluctant to give up his seat when Roosevelt asked him to run for vice president in 1944. But in the end he did accept the nomination, and he was elevated to the oval office on the death of Roosevelt on April 12, 1945. For a time, he enjoyed a favorable position with the Republican-controlled Congress. But the honeymoon was short-lived, and he came under criticism by Congress for both his actions and his sometimes off-the-cuff remarks and salty language. But as time passed, his confidence grew to the point where he decided to run for the office himself in 1948. His stunning "upset" (according to all pre-election polls) remains today one of the strangest of all elections of a president of the United States. In the end, historians rank him as one of America's better presidents.

Truman was born in 1884 in the family home in Lamar, Missouri. The S was his complete middle name, so there is no period after the initial as there is with other presidents. His father was a farmer and livestock salesman who later in life became an election judge and road overseer. His mother grew up in a pro-Confederate household during the Civil War and never quite forgave the Yankees for their treatment of her family during the war. She once visited her son in the White House but refused to sleep in the Lincoln Bedroom.

Truman's childhood was spent on family farms in various parts of Missouri; he eventually established solid roots in Independence. Young Harry wore thick glasses as a child, so his parents did not allow him to engage in strenuous sporting activities. He admitted to being something of a sissy as a youth and preferred playing piano to baseball. His mother taught him to read, but he did attend public schools in Independence. When he decided on seeking a career in politics, he enrolled at Kansas City Law School. At the age of 35, he married Elizabeth "Bess" Virginia Wallace. She would later resent his becoming vice president and did not enjoy her years as First Lady at all.

During World War I, Truman served with the 129th Field Artillery, where he rose from the rank of lieutenant to that of major. His political career began in 1922 when he was elected judge of Jackson County, Missouri. His political backer was Thomas J. Pendergast, leader of a powerful (and sometimes corrupt) political machine. After serving a number of terms as a judge, he was elected to the United States Senate from Missouri, again getting most of his political support from Pendergast. While he admitted that part of the reason for his election was the powerful Kansas City political machine controlled by Pendergast,

Truman himself was always honest and his integrity was never questioned. He dearly loved his seat in the Senate and was successfully reelected in 1940. When Roosevelt asked him to serve as his running mate in 1944, Truman declined because he much preferred being a senator to being vice president. In the end Roosevelt convinced him to join the party ticket. Not long after Roosevelt's fourth term began, he died, and Truman became president.

ELECTION OF 1948

During the early stages of the 1948 Democratic convention, few believed that Truman had much of a chance of being elected in his own right. Therefore, they courted the popular war hero Dwight D. Eisenhower, whose political affiliation at that point was uncommitted. When Eisenhower declined, support began to shift to Truman, who surprisingly was nominated on the first ballot over the Southern Conservative choice of Richard Russell. The Republicans nominated Thomas E. Dewey as their choice with Governor Earl Warren of California as their choice for vice president. Strom Thurmond of South Carolina represented the Dixiecrats (Southern Democrats) and Henry Wallace ran on the Progressive ticket.

1. Most people had written off Harry Truman as a "caretaker president doomed to defeat." What do you think was meant by this statement?

   _____

   _____

2. Despite being a decided underdog, Truman embarked on a vigorous 30,000-mile "whistlestop campaign" in which he delivered more than 300 speeches. What is meant by the term *whistlestop campaign*?

   _____

   _____

   _____

3. As election day approached, Truman was literally given no chance to win. All three of the major polls (Gallup, Roper, and Crossley) predicted victory for Dewey. One Chicago newspaper even sent out its early morning edition the morning after the election with the headline "Dewey Defeats Truman." We all know it did not turn out that way! Some say that is why we have elections. Research the results and record them on the back of this sheet. Then explain the unlikelihood that pollsters will ever make a mistake like this again.

DWIGHT D. EISENHOWER

★ ★

Courtesy Library of Congress

He described himself as a conservative, "but an extremely liberal conservative." During the '50s everybody "liked Ike" as the nation elected the popular war hero as president in both 1952 and 1956. He had risen to the rank of five-star general, the highest rank the U.S. Army had to bestow. He was proud of this, and he was also proud of being elected as president of the United States, but he never became "stuffed shirty," an image he wanted to avoid. War heroes do not always make good presidents, but the American public begged him to run. When he did finally accept, he was elected by a wide margin.

He was born in 1890 in a rented room near the railroad tracks in Denison, Texas. His father was a mechanic, then a store owner until the store went bankrupt, and finally the manager of a gas company. His mother was a deeply religious pacifist who was against her son enrolling at West Point.

Eisenhower's early years were spent in Abilene, Kansas, where his family moved when he was still an infant. When he was very young, he began peddling produce from the family garden and shoveling coal to make money. When he was 15, he developed blood poisoning following a knee injury. Doctors wanted to amputate, but Eisenhower said he would rather die than have his leg cut off. He developed an early interest in military history, but he really wanted to become a railroad engineer when he grew up.

After attending public schools in Abilene, he entered the U.S. Military Academy at West Point. There he played on the football team until a knee injury forced him to abandon his football career. Upon graduation from West Point, he began his career as a professional soldier. During World War I, he remained in the United States as a training instructor. When the war was over, he remained in the army, serving in various capacities that moved him up the ladder to brigadier general. When the United States became involved in World War II, he was appointed commander of the U.S. forces in Europe and later Allied commander in chief of the invasion of North Africa. In 1943 he was named by President Roosevelt as the supreme Allied commander, with orders to mount an invasion of Europe aimed at Germany. His successful invasion at Normandy landed him a promotion to the rank of five-star general. He led the final assault on Germany in 1945 and accepted the German surrender. He then served briefly as president of Columbia University and was appointed by President Truman as the chief of NATO.

ELECTION OF 1952
When the Republicans gathered in July of 1952, almost everyone "liked Ike," the popular war hero. He was nominated on the first ballot with Richard Nixon chosen as his running mate. The Democrats chose Adlai E. Stevenson of Illinois as their man for president and John Sparkman of Alabama for vice president.

1. While there were other issues in the campaign, the main focus centered on the personalities of the two candidates. Also, television was used in the campaigns for the first time. Research the history behind this election and report on the images the two candidates portrayed before the American public by the time Election Day rolled around.

_____

_____

_____

ELECTION OF 1956

In 1956 the Republicans did not hesitate to renominate their popular incumbent president. Even though Stevenson had not come close in the election of 1952, the Democrats renominated him on the first ballot. Senator Estes Kefauver won the nomination for vice president over Senator John F. Kennedy. The Republicans again chose Richard Nixon to run for vice president.

2. In reality, Stevenson stood little chance of unseating the popular Eisenhower. However, he mounted the best campaign effort he could muster, considering the circumstances. Find out the significance of the famous photo of Stevenson with a hole in his shoe and how the Republicans used the photo in their campaign.

_____

_____

3. The Democrats attempted to capitalize on the heart attack that President Eisenhower had suffered during his first term in office, citing this as a good reason for not electing him a second time. How did Ike respond to this charge?

_____

_____

4. One of the campaign bumper stickers used by the Democrats exclaimed "Hogan for President!" Find out the meaning and implications associated with this campaign slogan.

_____

_____

JOHN F. KENNEDY

★ ★

Courtesy The White House

He was young; he was handsome; he was articulate; he portrayed the image of the successful and ideal leader Americans wanted during the early 1960s. Kennedy overcame a number of health tragedies and won the purple heart for his heroics on the PT-109. Later, his romance-filled marriage to the attractive Jacqueline Bouvier made them the couple of mythical Camelot.

He was the first president born in the twentieth century. He was born in 1917 in Brookline, Massachusetts. His father, Joseph, a Harvard graduate and millionaire by the time he was 35, made money at virtually everything he chose to do. His ventures into the stock market, the real estate market, Hollywood movies, and the Securities and Exchange Commission made him one of America's most prosperous businessmen. His mother, Rose, also came from wealth. John F. (better known as Jack to his friends) was second of nine Kennedy children.

His youth was spent in the comforts of Brookline, Massachusetts, New York City, and the family summer home in Hyannis Port, Cape Cod, Massachusetts. He was educated in the finest schools and, although a scrawny youth because of his many illnesses, was a scrapper and a good athlete. At Harvard University, he majored in political science and played on the football and golf teams. Upon graduating cum laude from Harvard, he enrolled in the Stanford Business School.

He volunteered for the army in 1941, but he failed the physical because of his bad back. His father influenced the navy into getting him command of the PT-109. During his service as skipper, the boat was destroyed by a Japanese vessel and Kennedy was thrown into the sea. He swam for over four hours, towing an injured crewman with him, and was eventually rescued on an island in the Pacific. For his heroic deeds, he was awarded the purple heart and the Marine Corps medal. The event was widely publicized and gained national attention in the media.

His political career began with his election to Congress as representative from the Eleventh Congressional District in Massachusetts. He was reelected twice more to the post until he successfully won election to the U.S. Senate in 1952. Although he was a rich man himself, he gained a reputation as a champion of the common man. In 1956 he was one of the hopefuls for the vice-presidential nomination, but he did not win the nomination.

ELECTION OF 1960

By the time the Democratic convention began in 1960, Kennedy had emerged as the number-one choice to win the nomination for president. He did this on the first ballot and chose Lyndon B. Johnson as his running mate. The Republicans banked on Vice President Richard Nixon to win the presidency and chose Henry Cabot Lodge as their vice-presidential candidate.

1. The pre-election polls indicated an extremely tight race with the lead seesawing back and forth as the campaign wore on. One of Kennedy's main themes was to denounce the Eisenhower administration for allowing communism to rise to power less than 90 miles from the United States in Cuba. Nixon hammered on Kennedy's youth and limited experience in government. The Republican Party also emphasized Kennedy's association with the Catholic church, implying the danger that a Catholic president might be answering to the Vatican on certain issues. Find out how Kennedy credited his eventual razor-close win to the four television debates which the two engaged in during the campaign.

   _____

   _____

   _____

2. The popular vote was extremely close! Research the results of the election and express the margin of Kennedy's victory as a percent.

   _____

   _____

3. How did Dr. Martin Luther King, Jr.'s father help to swing the black vote over to Kennedy?

   _____

   _____

   _____

LYNDON B. JOHNSON

★ ★

Courtesy Library of Congress

He might have been one of America's greatest presidents had it not been for Vietnam. Despite the unpopularity of the war in Vietnam, Johnson is still regarded as one of America's most efficient politicians and presidents with a reputation for "getting the job done." He was the first real Southerner since Woodrow Wilson to become president, and he was the first "real Texan" to occupy the White House. His folksy Southern charm, homespun advice from "what my Daddy told me," and his uncanny ability to manipulate people to get what he wanted were sometimes offset by his quick temper that led to sudden outrage, a very strong ego, and a sometimes too-high opinion of himself. He became president during that bitter day in 1963 when President Kennedy was assassinated in Dallas, and he guided the nation out of that period of doubt on to a course of rediscovery.

Johnson was born in 1908 in a three-room farmhouse near Johnson City, Texas. His father was a farmer turned cotton broker and later a legislator who strongly opposed the Ku Klux Klan. His mother was a teacher and editor of a small local newspaper.

As a child, Johnson grew up in hard times. He did whatever odd jobs were available to earn extra money. Johnson attended public schools in Johnson City, where he also took dance lessons and engaged in school debates. He worked his way through Southwest Texas Teachers College. Upon graduation, he studied law briefly at Georgetown University. In 1934 he married "Lady Bird" Taylor.

Johnson's political career began with his winning a special election for the House seat from the Tenth Congressional District in Texas. He was reelected to the House six times. His next step up the ladder was to win election to the U.S. Senate in 1949, where he became a powerful leader in the Democratic Party. During the 1960 Democratic National Convention, he was a leading contender for the presidential nomination, and people were surprised when he accepted Kennedy's invitation to run for vice president. When President Kennedy was assassinated that fateful morning in Dallas, Johnson was in the same motorcade, riding two cars behind President Kennedy's limousine. He took the oath of office just a few hours later.

ELECTION OF 1964
Because Johnson had proven himself to be a strong leader while he finished Kennedy's term of office, the Democrats nominated him by acclamation at their convention in 1964. The vice-presidential nomination went to Hubert H. Humphrey of Minnesota. The Republicans chose ultra-conservative Barry Goldwater of Arizona as their nominee for president and William Miller of New York as his running mate.

1. Johnson remained somewhat aloof during the campaign. He really did not need to get too involved. In fact, he declined Goldwater's challenge to debate. Goldwater spread his "freedom of association" plan for America far and wide. Find out about Goldwater's campaign and what he really meant by this phrase.

_____
_____
_____
_____
_____

2. Goldwater's campaign slogan was "In your heart, you know he's right." The Democrats countered with "In your heart, you know he might." What do you think the Democrats meant by this statement?

_____
_____
_____

3. In the end, the voters of America overwhelmingly chose Johnson. Research the election results and record both the popular vote and the electoral vote in the space below. Express the results also as percentages.

_____
_____
_____

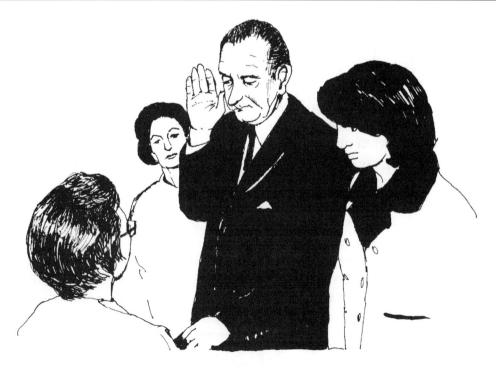

RICHARD M. NIXON

★ ★

He was the first president ever to resign while in office. He was also one of the most elusive and controversial of all presidents. He even acquired the nickname "Tricky Dick" for his often-secret and furtive antics. The resignation of his vice president, Spiro Agnew, who was caught on bribery and income tax evasion charges, was only the beginning of Nixon's downfall. The Watergate scandal involving the burglary of the Democratic headquarters during the 1972 presidential campaign was eventually traced back to Nixon's authorization, and his presidency began to unravel. When the House of Representatives began the procedures to vote for actual articles of impeachment against him, Nixon finally resigned. His resignation remains one of the darkest days of the U.S. presidency.

Richard Milhaus Nixon was born in 1913 in the small frame house his father had built in Yorba Linda, California. His father owned a gas station for a time and later became a house painter and odd-jobs man. His mother was a devout Quaker. Young Richard grew up in poverty in Yorba Linda and volunteered for any jobs he could find to earn extra money.

He attended public schools in Yorba Linda and Whittier, California. He decided at an early age that he wanted to become a lawyer. After finishing high school, he enrolled at Whittier College and later Duke University Law School, where he graduated. Shortly thereafter, he was admitted to the bar.

Nixon practiced law for a time and then joined the navy. When he was discharged, he decided to run for Congress and won, representing California's Twelfth Congressional District. While he was in Congress, he earned a reputation for his dogged pursuit of Communist spies in America. In 1950 he won a seat in the United States Senate. Then in 1952, Republican nominee for president Dwight D. Eisenhower chose him as his running mate to become vice president. After serving under Eisenhower for eight years, he ran for president in 1960 against John F. Kennedy. He lost in one of the closest presidential races ever. Then Nixon ran for governor of California and he lost again. Many thought Richard Nixon's political career was over. Those who thought so were wrong.

ELECTION OF 1968

When the Republican convention began in 1968 in Miami Beach, Richard Nixon's name had once again risen to the surface. In fact, he was nominated on the first ballot. His running mate was Governor Spiro Agnew of Maryland. The Democrats chose Hubert Humphrey of Minnesota and Edmund Muskie of Maine. George Wallace of Alabama ran as a third-party candidate on the American Independent Party ticket.

1. Part of the problem for the Democratic campaign in 1968 was the violence that had erupted during the convention in Chicago. Find out what caused the violence and also how the unpopularity of the Johnson administration concerning the war in Vietnam contributed to the undoing of any chances Humphrey might have had to win.

_____

_____

_____

_____

ELECTION OF 1972

The Republicans immediately renominated Nixon and Agnew at their convention, again in Miami Beach, in 1972. The Democrats chose Senator George McGovern of South Dakota and Thomas Eagleton of Missouri. However, it was discovered that Eagleton had undergone shock therapy for mental depression, and Eagleton resigned from the race for the good of the party. McGovern then chose Sargent Shriver of Maryland as his new running mate.

2. George McGovern was regarded by many American voters as a "radical leftist." Research this campaign and explain the reasons why McGovern, who was indeed a man of principle, ran one of the poorest races ever in the history of the American presidency. Why do you think he lost by such a wide margin?

_____

_____

_____

_____

GERALD R. FORD

★ ★

Courtesy Library of Congress, Prints and Photographs Division [LC-USZ62-13038]

Gerald R. Ford was the first man to become president by appointment rather than by election. Appointed vice president by President Nixon when Spiro Agnew resigned in disgrace, he became the first vice president appointed under the provisions of the Twenty-Fifth Amendment. He then became our nation's president when Nixon himself resigned under threat of impeachment. Ford's personality has been described as good-natured, easy-going, and unpretentious. He had very few enemies. His many years as a leader in Congress made him well-respected by his colleagues. He was extremely disappointed when he lost the election of 1976 in a close race to Jimmy Carter, because he felt he had done a good job as president and deserved to be elected in his own right.

He was born Leslie Lynch King, Jr., in 1913 in Omaha, Nebraska. The tempestuous marriage of his parents lasted only three years, and Ford remembers seeing his father only twice. He remained bitter and always resented his biological father for not being there when he was needed. His name was changed to Gerald R. Ford, Jr., after his adoptive father when his mother remarried. Ford had a genuinely wonderful relationship with his adoptive father and always held him in the highest esteem.

Ford grew up in Grand Rapids, Michigan, performing the typical chores that were expected of a young boy. He loved being a member of the Boy Scouts and rose to the rank of Eagle Scout. He attended public schools in Grand Rapids and, upon graduation, entered the University of Michigan. He became an outstanding football player there and was sought by a number of professional teams after graduation. Instead he entered Yale Law School, where he eventually graduated and was admitted to the Michigan bar.

He began a law practice in Grand Rapids but joined the navy during World War II. His military career earned him no fewer than ten battle stars! When the war was over, Gerald Ford ran for Congress and was elected from Michigan's Fifth Congressional District. Ford was reelected to Congress 12 times in succession and, during his many years, he emerged as a powerful leader of several important committees. He always had wanted to become House Speaker, but at that time Congress was controlled by the Democrats, so it seemed that this would never happen. Thus, early in 1973 he decided to run for Congress one more time and then retire at the end of his term of office in 1976. History would change his plan.

His appointment as vice president and elevation to the office of the presidency without ever facing the test of an election gave Gerald Ford a unique and somewhat strange place in American history.

1. Within minutes of the resignation of Richard Nixon, Ford was administered the oath of office. Shortly thereafter, he issued a full pardon to Nixon, hoping to heal the nation's wounds. He was criticized for doing this by many who thought it unfair to pardon Nixon when many of those who acted on his behalf were punished. What is your opinion? Research the Watergate incident and explain your feelings about Ford's granting a full pardon to former President Nixon. Be certain to justify your feelings.

_____

_____

_____

_____

2. Read the text of the Twenty-Fifth Amendment to the Constitution. Explain the importance of the amendment to our national security and well-being as a nation. What did Gerald Ford do about having a vice president when he became president?

_____

_____

_____

_____

3. While many people said good things about "Jerry" Ford and no one ever doubted his integrity, former President Lyndon B. Johnson once said, "He's a nice fellow, but he spent too much time playing football without a helmet." He was also criticized by Ronald Reagan, who claimed that ". . . under Ford, the nation has become number two in military power in a world where it is dangerous—if not fatal—to be second best." Explain what these two men meant by their criticisms of Ford.

_____

_____

_____

_____

JIMMY CARTER

★ ★

Courtesy Library of Congress, Prints and Photographs Division [LC-US262-13039]

When Jimmy Carter announced that he was running for president in December of 1974, he was relatively unknown outside his own state of Georgia, where he was governor. In fact, during that same year, he appeared on a TV show called *What's My Line?* and he almost stumped the panel. But by announcing his candidacy early, Jimmy Carter had plenty of time to quietly build his following. He won a few early victories in the Democratic primaries, and his support began to swell. Carter was a born-again Christian and a deeply religious man. His critics claimed he lacked a sense of humor, but many Americans found him refreshing. He became the first man from the Deep South to be elected president since Zachary Taylor in 1848. His southern charm and unpretentious manners, combined with his commitment to ensuring the successful administration of civil rights measures passed during the 1960s, could not offset his perceived failure at foreign policy. So those in the business of rating the effectiveness of presidents often place him in the category of "less than average."

He was born James Earl Carter, Jr., in a hospital in Plains, Georgia, in 1924. He was the first president to be born in a hospital. His father was a farmer, a peanut broker, and later a public official. He eventually amassed a farm of over 4,000 acres that was tended by 200 tenant farmers. His mother, Lillian, supported racial equality long before it was an acceptable practice. At the age of 68, she even joined the Peace Corps and spent two years doing volunteer work in India. She visited the White House often during Jimmy Carter's years as president, and she enjoyed her role as "First Mother."

Carter's early childhood was spent in Archery, Georgia, a largely black community. He was allowed to play with the black children, but he attended segregated schools and church services. At the age of five, he was selling boiled peanuts on the streets of Plains, Georgia. After attending public schools in Plains, he enrolled at Georgia Southwestern College. He then applied to the U.S. Naval Academy at Annapolis and graduated near the top of his class. He intended to make the navy his career.

Shortly after graduation from Annapolis, he married Rosalynn Smith, a native of Plains, who was thrilled with the excitement of traveling with her husband as a navy wife. When Carter's father died in 1953, Jimmy resigned his commission and returned home to manage the Carter peanut business, much to the disappointment of his wife. Rosalynn became his bookkeeper, and the two turned the business into a prosperous enterprise. In 1962 he decided to run for the Georgia state senate. He was reelected two years later and then ran unsuccessfully to become governor of Georgia in 1966. He came back in 1970, and this time he won the governorship.

ELECTION OF 1976

By the time the Democrats gathered in New York for their convention, Jimmy Carter had risen from being relatively unknown to becoming the leading contender for the nomination. He won on the first ballot and chose Senator Walter Mondale of Minnesota as his running mate. The Republicans chose Ford for president and Senator Robert Dole of Kansas as his running mate.

1. When the campaign began, President Ford was nearly 30 percentage points behind Jimmy Carter. By election day, the race was "too close to call." Research the issues that became the focus of this campaign and report the stand of each party on each issue.

    national health insurance—

    Democrats _____

    Republicans _____

    expenditures for national defense—

    Democrats _____

    Republicans _____

    abortion—

    Democrats _____

    Republicans _____

    control of the Panama Canal—

    Democrats _____

    Republicans _____

    busing students to achieve racial equality in schools—

    Democrats _____

    Republicans _____

2. The election of 1976 was indeed a close race. Look at the results and explain the demographics of the election in terms of those areas of the country won by each candidate.

    Deep South- _____

    Industrial North- _____

    West-_____

RONALD REAGAN

★ ★

He was the oldest of our presidents at 69 years of age when he was elected, and he was almost 78 when he retired from office. He was also the only professional actor to become president. His Hollywood career included 54 films, many of them considered quality films. He was considered a "very good actor" by Hollywood standards and won special praise for his performances in *Brother Rat, Knute Rockne—All American,* and *King's Row*. His years before that as a radio sportscaster were important to him because he was doing what he wanted to do. World War II interrupted his movie career and, when he returned, he found himself relegated to less-than-desirable roles. As his Hollywood career began to decline, he turned to television and served as host of *General Electric Theater* and later as host of the half-hour television series *Death Valley Days*. Reagan always loved his career in Hollywood as well as his days in radio and television. But when he turned to politics, he said his past seemed as dull as dishwater, compared to the world of politics.

Ronald Reagan was born in 1911 in a five-room house in Tampico, Illinois. His father was a shoe salesman, working for a time for Marshall Field's in Chicago. He suffered from bouts with alcoholism. Young Ronald's mother always took great care to ensure that her children realized that their father's alcoholism was a disease, for which they should not resent him.

Reagan's childhood was spent in a number of Illinois communities, including Chicago, Galesburg, Monmouth, Tampico, and Dixon. As a boy, he worked digging foundations for houses and as a roustabout when the circus came to town. After graduation from Dixon High School, he enrolled at Eureka College, where he majored in economics, played on the football team, and was a member of the swimming and track teams. Following graduation, he decided to pursue a career in radio broadcasting. He used radio as a steppingstone to a career in Hollywood. After passing his screen test, he began a career in motion pictures that spanned nearly 30 years.

After the decline of his movie career, he turned to television, and then he served as cochairman of the California Republicans for Barry Goldwater in 1964. He did a 30-minute television address on behalf of Goldwater, which drew more contributions than any speech in history. In 1966 he was elected governor of California over incumbent Pat Brown, who was seeking a third term. As governor, he gained a nationwide reputation for frugal and wise spending and was able to restore the state to solvency by overcoming the extreme financial difficulties he had inherited when he took office. He attempted to win the Republican nomination in 1976 but lost to Gerald Ford.

ELECTION OF 1980

While Reagan faced opposition at the Republican convention in Detroit, he was nominated on the first ballot. He wanted former President Ford to run as his vice-presidential candidate, but Ford declined, so Reagan chose George Bush of Texas. The Democrats quickly renominated incumbent President Jimmy Carter and Vice President Walter Mondale. John R. Anderson of Illinois ran on the Independent Party ticket for president.

1. From the outset of the campaign, President Carter knew he was in trouble. Many of his problems were traced back to the list of promises he had made to the American public when he asked them to elect him in 1976. Republicans pointed to his list and cited all the many promises he had made that had failed to materialize. Research this election and identify some of those unfulfilled promises that led to the landslide victory of Ronald Reagan in 1980.

   _____

   _____

   _____

   _____

ELECTION OF 1984

By the time the 1984 election rolled around, President Reagan faced literally no opposition at all in his bid for renomination. Both Reagan and Vice President Bush were nominated together in a single roll-call vote on the first ballot. The Democrats chose Walter Mondale for president and Mondale in turn chose Geraldine Ferraro of New York as his running mate. Ferraro became the first woman on a major party ticket.

2. Deficit spending, foreign trade, and Reagan's age were the major issues surrounding the campaign of 1984. Find out how the traditional roles of the Democratic and Republican parties seemed almost reversed during this campaign on the following two issues. Identify the position each party had normally taken on each issue and how the two candidates stood on each issue. Use the reverse side of this sheet to explain your findings.

   Deficit Spending: traditional Democratic position vs. that of Mondale; traditional Republican position vs. that of Reagan

   Foreign Trade: traditional Democratic position vs. that of Mondale; traditional Republican position vs. that of Reagan

GEORGE BUSH

★★★★★★★★★★★★★★★★★★★★★★★★★

When people voted for George Bush during the election of 1988, many were not exactly certain what they were getting. Was Bush a Connecticut Yankee or was he a good old boy from Texas? Was he a New England patrician or a regular guy from the Southwest? He had come from both backgrounds and also brought with him a string of political appointments and offices that added a lot of credibility to his being a candidate for president. As Reagan's vice president for two terms, Bush had quietly served the wishes of his boss. His early type-A personality as an oilman had been altered by health problems, and as president he became a more gentle man who would rather talk than fight.

George Herbert Walker Bush was born in 1924 in the family Victorian home in Milton, Massachusetts. His father, Prescott S. Bush, was a successful investment banker who eventually won election to the United States Senate, representing the state of Connecticut. Bush's father set extremely high standards for all of his children, and Bush's mother, a remarkable athlete and strict disciplinarian herself, instilled in her children a love of sports.

Bush's childhood was spent in the comforts of Greenwich Country Day School. For a time young George was enrolled in the prestigious Phillips Academy in Andover, Massachusetts. While there, George participated in a number of extracurricular activities, including playing on the baseball and soccer teams, being president of the senior class, and presiding over the Society of Inquiry. When Bush graduated, he planned to enroll at Yale University, but military service interrupted his education. He enlisted in the navy and eventually earned his wings, becoming the youngest pilot in the navy. On one occasion, he was shot down over the Pacific and remained in the water for more than three hours before he was rescued.

When he left the military, he enrolled at Yale University, where he majored in economics and also played first base on the baseball team. Upon graduation with honors, Bush decided to learn the oil business. He moved to Texas and rose through the ranks, prospering financially along the way. By the early 1950s, George Bush had become interested in politics. Even though he continued his oil interests, he served in a variety of capacities within the Republican Party in Texas, and in 1964 he sought election to the U.S. Senate. He lost the election, but the seed of political office was now firmly planted within him.

In 1966 he won election to Congress as the representative from the Seventh Congressional District in Texas. He won reelection two years later and then decided to run for U.S. Senate. He lost that election as well, but a number of important political appointments followed: President Nixon appointed him as U.S. ambassador to the United Nations in 1971; Nixon then named him chairman of the Republican National Committee in 1973; President Nixon named him chief U.S. liaison in China; then Ford named him director of the Central Intelligence Agency in 1976. He was Ronald Reagan's choice as his running mate during the election of 1980 and again in 1984.

ELECTION OF 1988

Bush's vast background in government and politics made him the obvious choice of the Republicans when they met in New Orleans in 1988, and he was nominated on the first ballot. His choice for running mate was Senator Dan Quayle of Indiana. The Democrats chose Michael S. Dukakis of Massachusetts, and Senator Lloyd Bentsen of Texas as his running mate.

1. The campaign itself was one of the most negative in recent history, with both candidates taking shots at each other rather than focusing on what should have been the issues of the campaign. Research the election and find out what each candidate claimed he would accomplish if elected president.

GEORGE BUSH   MICHAEL DUKAKIS

_____   _____
_____   _____
_____   _____
_____   _____
_____   _____

2. Research the results of the election and find out the demographics of the following:

Who won the male vote? _____

Who won the female vote? _____

Who won the black vote? _____

How many popular votes did Bush get? _____

How many did Dukakis get? _____

How many electoral votes did Bush get? _____

How many did Dukakis get? _____

BILL CLINTON

★ ★

Courtesy Library of Congress, Prints and Photographs Division [LC-USZ62-107700]

He was born William Jefferson Blythe, IV, named after his father, who had been tragically killed in an automobile accident just before his son was born. At the age of 16, he legally changed his last name to Clinton (that of his stepfather) in an effort to cement a very strained relationship. From the time he had the honor of shaking hands with President Kennedy, he decided he wanted to follow a career in politics, though he was a gifted musician, and many others thought his calling was that of a minister.

Clinton was born in 1946 at Julia Chester Hospital in Hope, Arkansas, the son of a successful traveling salesman engaged in selling heavy construction equipment. Since his company was based in Chicago, he had bought a house there and was on his way to pick up his wife when the accident occurred near Sikeston, Missouri. Throughout his life, Clinton was haunted by the specter of a father he never knew. His mother was a nurse anesthetist who remarried a few years after her husband's death. Her husband, Roger Clinton, was an abusive alcoholic who brought misery to both young Bill and his mother. She eventually divorced him but later remarried him out of pity.

Much of Clinton's early childhood was spent with his maternal grandparents in Hope while his mother advanced her nurse's training in New Orleans. The entire extended family of aunts, uncles, and cousins was closely knit and took great interest in all children. At the age of seven, his mother and stepfather moved the family to Hot Springs, where he spent the remainder of his youth. He loved being a Boy Scout, singing in the church choir, and playing the saxophone. He won a trip to Washington, D.C., as a "senator" from Arkansas in the American Legion program Boys' Nation. In a reception on the White House lawn, he got to shake hands with President Kennedy, an event that had a profound effect on his life.

After graduating fourth in his class of 323 from Hot Springs High School, Clinton enrolled at Georgetown University. Upon graduating with a degree in international affairs, he began study as a Rhodes scholar at Oxford University in England. While a student there, he took steps to avoid the draft during the Vietnam War, which he strongly opposed. After two years there, he returned to the United States, enrolled at Yale University law school, and earned his law degree. He then accepted an offer to teach law at the University of Arkansas law school. In 1975 he married Hillary Rodham, who had also earned a law degree. She kept her maiden name for a number of years until the pressure of her husband's political career seemed to warrant reference to her as "Mrs. Clinton."

Clinton worked very hard within the Democratic Party, quietly waiting for his chance to step into politics. After a few minor setbacks, he successfully won election to become attorney general of Arkansas in 1976. In 1979 he won election as the state's governor. Two years later he was defeated for reelection, but he won the office again in 1982 and remained the state's governor until 1992.

ELECTION OF 1992

Clinton won the Democratic nomination on the first ballot. He chose Al Gore as his running mate. The Republicans quickly renominated President Bush and Dan Quayle. Ross Perot, a Texas billionaire, was a very strong third-party candidate on the Independent ticket.

1. The campaign of 1992 was a most unusual one in that it boiled down to a simple referendum on President Bush. Never had the fortunes of an incumbent president fallen so far so fast. And it had been a good many years since a third-party candidate had won such a large percentage of the popular vote. Research the results of the election and report both the popular vote and the electoral vote.

_____

_____

_____

ELECTION OF 1996

Clinton and Gore faced no real challenges at the 1996 Democratic convention and were renominated without opposition. The Republicans chose former Senator Bob Dole of Kansas and Jack Kemp of New York as his running mate. Ross Perot again ran as an independent candidate. The Green Party was represented by consumer advocate Ralph Nader.

2. Both candidates launched vigorous campaigns, spending thousands of hours and miles trying to influence voters. Their running mates were equally ambitious. In the end the public chose to remain with the status quo and reelected their Democratic president. Look at the election results and compare Clinton's win in 1996 with his win in 1992.

_____

_____

_____

3. In 1998 William Jefferson Clinton was impeached by the House of Representatives, making him only the second president in American history to be impeached. Research the charges that were brought against him. In your opinion, were those charges serious enough to merit impeachment? Should he have been removed from office?

_____

_____

_____

Test your knowledge of those who became president including the campaigns, the elections, and the other circumstances that elevated them to the Oval Office. Each item is followed by the names of three presidents. Only one is correct. All 12 of the questions in this "skill check" were taken from material found in the profile assignments you completed on the presidents. If you know your American history, the two incorrect possibilities will be pretty easy to rule out. After completing your quiz, check your answers and find out the correct answer for any you may have missed.

1. _____ He became the first vice president to accede to the presidency on the death of a president.
        a. John Adams
        b. Andrew Jackson
        c. John Tyler

2. _____ He was the first president to win an election in which voting took place throughout the nation on the same day.
        a. Zachary Taylor
        b. Woodrow Wilson
        c. Calvin Coolidge

3. _____ He followed Millard Fillmore into the White House and was himself succeeded by James Buchanan.
        a. Thomas Jefferson
        b. James Polk
        c. Franklin Pierce

4. _____ He was the first dark-horse candidate to be nominated by a major party.
        a. James Monroe
        b. James Polk
        c. Martin Van Buren

5. _____ He was considered a traitor in the North, as he was the only president to join the Confederacy.
        a. John Adams
        b. John Tyler
        c. William McKinley

6. _____ He was immensely popular following his military success during World War II, and his popularity carried him into the White House in the election of 1952.
   a. Woodrow Wilson
   b. Dwight D. Eisenhower
   c. Lyndon B. Johnson

7. _____ History ranks him as our greatest president.
   a. George Washington
   b. Abraham Lincoln
   c. Theodore Roosevelt

8. _____ This campaign slogan caught on and helped him win the election of 1840: "Tippecanoe and Tyler, Too!"
   a. William Henry Harrison
   b. James Buchanan
   c. William Howard Taft

9. _____ His surprise win over Thomas Dewey in 1948 was proof enough that polls do not determine who wins elections. The voters do!
   a. Warren G. Harding
   b. Harry Truman
   c. Jimmy Carter

10. _____ He was elected president just before the bad times hit America when the stock market crashed in 1929.
    a. Zachary Taylor
    b. Ulysses S. Grant
    c. Herbert Hoover

11. _____ He has been the only president who was once a movie star. His popularity as governor of California helped to propel him into the White House in the election of 1980.
    a. James Polk
    b. Franklin D. Roosevelt
    c. Ronald Reagan

12. _____ He has been the only president to remain a bachelor.
    a. James Buchanan
    b. Warren G. Harding
    c. Grover Cleveland

10–12 correct: Campaign Chairman   8–11 correct: Party Leader
4–7 correct: Party "Footsoldier"   0–3 correct: Better Suited for Other Work

Test your knowledge of those who became president including the campaigns, the elections, and the other circumstances that elevated them to the Oval Office. Each item is followed by the names of three presidents. Only one is correct. All 12 of the questions in this "skill check" were taken from material found in the profile assignments you completed on the presidents. If you know your American history, the two incorrect possibilities will be pretty easy to rule out. After making your choices, check your answers and find out the correct answer for any you may have missed. Use the same evaluation scale as you used in Election Trivia I.

1. _____ In the election of 1896, while his Democratic opponent, William Jennings Bryan, traveled over 18,000 miles and addressed over 5 million people, this Canton, Ohio, Republican conducted a "front porch campaign," yet still easily won the election.
   a. Franklin Pierce
   b. William McKinley
   c. Herbert Hoover

2. _____ During the 1964 campaign, Republican candidate Barry Goldwater supported the position that Americans should enjoy "freedom of association," i.e., the "right to choose to associate with minorities or not." But voters decided it was "too conservative" a position and elected this Democrat by a landslide.
   a. Lyndon B. Johnson
   b. John F. Kennedy
   c. William Howard Taft

3. _____ He was elected president twice without opposition.
   a. George Washington
   b. John Adams
   c. Andrew Jackson

4. _____ He won the longest and most-disputed presidential election in our nation's history in 1876, when election fraud and a dispute over 20 electoral votes delayed the result for over four months!
   a. James Monroe
   b. Chester A. Arthur
   c. Rutherford B. Hayes

5. _____ He won election to the office of president in 1800 only after the election was thrown into the House of Representatives and 36 ballots were taken.
   a. Thomas Jefferson
   b. John Quincy Adams
   c. James Garfield

6. _____ He became the first president by appointment rather than by election.
   a. Dwight D. Eisenhower
   b. Gerald R. Ford
   c. Bill Clinton

7. _____ His exploits in the Civil War won him election as president in 1868.
   a. John Quincy Adams
   b. Ulysses S. Grant
   c. Theodore Roosevelt

8. _____ His election four times brought about the Twenty-second Amendment.
   a. Theodore Roosevelt
   b. Franklin D. Roosevelt
   c. Jimmy Carter

9. _____ He became the first president to resign while in office.
   a. Warren G. Harding
   b. Andrew Johnson
   c. Richard Nixon

10. _____ He was the first president to be impeached.
    a. Andrew Johnson
    b. Richard Nixon
    c. Bill Clinton

11. _____ He was elected president twice but not to successive terms.
    a. Grover Cleveland
    b. Theodore Roosevelt
    c. Ronald Reagan

12. _____ He won the election of 1912 when former President Theodore Roosevelt ran as a third-party candidate and pulled votes away from incumbent President William Howard Taft.
    a. Chester A. Arthur
    b. Woodrow Wilson
    c. Harry Truman

ELECTION TRIVIA III

Test your knowledge of those who became president including the campaigns, the elections, and the other circumstances that elevated them to the Oval Office. Each item is followed by the names of three presidents. Only one is correct. All 12 of the questions in this "skill check" were taken from material found in the profile assignments you completed on the presidents. If you know your American history, the two incorrect possibilities will be pretty easy to rule out. After making your choices, check your answers and find out the correct answer for any you may have missed.

1. _____ He won the election of 1824 even though he lost both the popular and electoral votes to Andrew Jackson. None of the four candidates had a majority of electors, so the election was decided by the House of Representatives.
    a. John Quincy Adams
    b. William Howard Taft
    c. Calvin Coolidge

2. _____ He won election as president in 1808, running on the endorsement of former President Thomas Jefferson, and then won again in 1812.
    a. John Adams
    b. James Madison
    c. Woodrow Wilson

3. _____ He became president when William McKinley was assassinated, but he won election in his own right in 1904.
    a. Theodore Roosevelt
    b. Franklin D. Roosevelt
    c. Warren G. Harding

4. _____ His father was our nation's second president.
    a. Benjamin Harrison
    b. Theodore Roosevelt
    c. John Quincy Adams

5. _____ He became president when James Garfield was assassinated and then wanted to run for president in his own right in 1884. However, he lost the nomination to James G. Blaine, who then lost the election to Grover Cleveland.
    a. Calvin Coolidge
    b. Chester Arthur
    c. William Howard Taft

6. _____ He upended incumbent Grover Cleveland in the election of 1888, despite losing the vote of the people.
   a. Millard Fillmore
   b. Benjamin Harrison
   c. Herbert Hoover

7. _____ He lost in a close election in 1960 to John F. Kennedy but came back to win the presidency in 1968 and again in 1972.
   a. Harry Truman
   b. Jimmy Carter
   c. Richard Nixon

8. _____ He won the election of 1920, but the Teapot Dome and other scandals rocked his administration.
   a. Warren G. Harding
   b. John Tyler
   c. Ronald Reagan

9. _____ This former governor of Arkansas won election to the White House in 1992 and won a second term in 1996.
   a. Jimmy Carter
   b. Bill Clinton
   c. Woodrow Wilson

10. _____ He was Ronald Reagan's VP before winning the presidency in 1988.
   a. Gerald Ford
   b. Lyndon B. Johnson
   c. George Bush

11. _____ He was so angry at losing the election of 1824, despite winning both the popular and electoral votes, that he announced his candidacy for the 1828 election almost immediately, and he won that election.
   a. Zachary Taylor
   b. Andrew Jackson
   c. James Buchanan

12. _____ This Democrat won in 1836 over William Henry Harrison, Hugh Lawson White, and Daniel Webster.
   a. Martin Van Buren
   b. Millard Fillmore
   c. William Howard Taft

Use the same evaluation scale you used for Election Trivia I and II to find out how much you really know about the campaigns and elections.

ANSWER KEY

★ ★

The President of the United States . . . page 2
1. Head of State—He is the living symbol of the United States. He should provide an inspiring example for the American people.
   Chief Foreign Policy Maker—He establishes foreign policy with help from his advisors and also decides how the United States will react to issues around the world.
   Chief Legislator—The president has a lot of influence in deciding which legislation will be passed.
   Chief of Party—He is his party's leader and thus must try to help others from his party to get elected.
   Watchdog of the Economy—He is in charge of the budget and should closely monitor the day-to-day events that affect the United States.
2. Answers will vary. John F. Kennedy was 43 years old when elected. Ronald Reagan was 69 years old when elected.
3. Presidents had limited themselves to two terms until Franklin D. Roosevelt, who was elected four times. The Twenty-second Amendment changed it to a limit of two terms or ten years maximum.

The Electoral College pages 3 and 4
1. Since the president was the man with the most votes and the vice president was the man with the second greatest number of votes, it often happened that the two men were political enemies. Yet they were supposed to get along and function as a team. There would be a natural resentment in the vice president toward the president in many cases. Also, under the original plan there was no distinction between the two electoral votes cast by each elector. He could not label one for president and one for vice president. Both votes were regarded as votes for the president.
2. The Twelfth Amendment provided for separate candidates from each party running for president and vice president. Each party's pair of candidates runs as a team.
3. In the election of 1800, Thomas Jefferson and Aaron Burr received the same number of votes, and the election went to the House of Representatives. It took 36 ballots there to finally break the tie in favor of Jefferson.
4. Everyone knew that the ballots for Jefferson were cast for him as president and those cast for Burr were intended to make him vice president. But since the votes could not be labeled and since Burr would not concede, the election went to the House of Representatives. The Twelfth Amendment of 1804 changed this so there are now separate candidates for president and vice president.
5. Today each party chooses its own slate of electors, who are pledged to vote the loyalty of their party.

Winning a Presidential Election pages 6–8

Alabama 9	Hawaii 4	Michigan 18	N. Carolina 14	Utah 5
Alaska 3	Idaho 4	Minnesota 10	N. Dakota 3	Vermont 3
Arizona 8	Illinois 22	Mississippi 7	Ohio 23	Virginia 13
Arkansas 6	Indiana 12	Missouri 11	Oklahoma 8	Washington 11
California 54	Iowa 7	Montana 3	Oregon 7	West Virginia 5
Colorado 8	Kansas 6	Nebraska 5	Pennsylvania 23	Wisconsin 11
Connecticut 8	Kentucky 8	Nevada 4	Rhode Island 4	Wyoming 3
Delaware 3	Louisiana 9	New Hampshire 4	S. Carolina 8	
Dist. of Col. 3	Maine 4	New Jersey 15	S. Dakota 3	
Florida 25	Maryland 10	New Mexico 5	Tennessee 11	
Georgia 13	Massachusetts 12	New York 33	Texas 32	

1. Answers will vary.
2. California 54, New York 33, Texas 32, Florida 25, Pennsylvania 23, Ohio 23
3. 538 ÷ 2 = 269 + 1 = 270
   190
4. Answers will vary, but it is extremely important for candidates to win as many of the populous states as they can. Thus, they spend more time and money on the more populous states.
5. Montana, Alaska, Wyoming, North Dakota, South Dakota, Vermont, Delaware, and Washington, D.C.
6. John Quincy Adams in 1824 vs. Andrew Jackson, Henry Clay, and William Crawford; James Polk in 1844 vs. Henry Clay; Zachary Taylor in 1848 vs. Lewis Cass and Martin Van Buren; James Buchanan in 1856 vs. John Fremont and Millard Fillmore; Abraham Lincoln in 1860 vs. Stephen Douglas, John Breckenridge, and John Bell; Rutherford B. Hayes in 1876 vs. Samuel Tilden; Benjamin Harrison in 1888 vs. Grover Cleveland; Grover Cleveland in 1892 vs. Benjamin Harrison and James Weaver; Woodrow Wilson in 1912 vs. Theodore Roosevelt and William H. Taft; Harry Truman in 1948 vs. Thomas Dewey, Strom Thurmond, and Henry Wallace; Richard Nixon in 1968 vs. Hubert Humphrey and George Wallace; Bill Clinton in 1992 vs. George Bush and Ross Perot
7. Answers will vary.
8. Answers will vary.
9. California 54, New York 33, Texas 32, Florida 25, Pennsylvania 23, Ohio 23, Illinois 22, Michigan 18, New Jersey 15, Virginia 13 (These ten states plus either Indiana 12 or Massachusetts 12 would give a candidate 270 electoral votes.)
10. Answers will vary.

Voting for Our President pages 9 and 10
Fourteenth Amendment—1868—gave 21-year-old males the right to vote even if they did not own property.
Fifteenth Amendment—1870—essentially gave blacks the right to vote, stating that the right to vote could not be denied "on account of race, color, or previous conditions of servitude."
Nineteenth Amendment—1920—gave women the right to vote—stating that voting rights cannot be denied "on account of sex."

Twenty-third Amendment—1961—gave the citizens of Washington, D.C., our nation's capital, the right to vote for their president even though they do not live in any state.
Twenty-fourth Amendment—1964—outlawed the poll tax as a condition of voting in federal elections. The tax had been created as a source of revenue in some of the southern states but in reality was aimed at keeping poor black people away from the polls.
Twenty-sixth Amendment—1971—lowered the voting age from 21 to 18 years of age.
1. Those under the age of 18
   Those who are not U.S. citizens
   Convicted felons and those who are severely mentally retarded
2. Answers will vary.
3. Answers will vary.

Political Parties in America pages 11–13
Answers will vary, but some general statements follow:
Democrats—
   Tend to be more liberal
   Tend to champion the cause of the common man
   Tend to lean more toward spending money on social programs than defense
Republicans—
   Tend to be more conservative
   Tend to be favored by big business and the wealthy
   Tend to spend more on military defense than on social programs
2. Answers will vary.
3. Answers will vary.
4. Answers will vary.
5. Depends on candidate chosen for research

The Road to the White House page 15
1. John Adams, Thomas Jefferson, Martin Van Buren, Theodore Roosevelt, Calvin Coolidge, Harry Truman, Lyndon Johnson, Richard Nixon, George Bush
2. George Washington 1792 — William McKinley 1900
   Thomas Jefferson 1804 — Woodrow Wilson 1916
   James Madison 1812 — Franklin D. Roosevelt 1936, 1940, 1944
   James Monroe 1820 — Dwight D. Eisenhower 1956
   Andrew Jackson 1832 — Richard Nixon 1972
   Abraham Lincoln 1864 — Ronald Reagan 1984
   Ulysses S. Grant 1872 — Bill Clinton 1996
3. John Quincy Adams 1828 — Gerald Ford 1976
   Martin Van Buren 1840 — Jimmy Carter 1980
   Grover Cleveland 1888 — George Bush 1992
   Herbert Hoover 1932
4. Answers will vary.

The Primaries page 17
1. New Hampshire
2. Voters are merely voting for the person they hope will represent their party best in the presidential election. They are not voting for a president during primary elections.
3. Answers will vary, but there is strong criticism that primaries serve little value beyond media hype.
4. Answers will vary.
5. Answers will vary.

The National Conventions pages 18 and 19
1. 1. Conventions establish rules for the selection of delegates and determining internal party policies.
   2. It places the party in the media limelight during the days of the convention. The hope is to gain exposure to voters.
   3. Each party determines its platform and develops position statements on important issues.
2. dark-horse candidate
3. Answers will vary.
4. Answers will vary.
5. Answers will vary.

The Vice-Presidential Candidate page 21
1. Thomas Jefferson was clearly the choice of the Republican Party. But since the Constitution gave each elector two votes and did not allow electors to determine which of their votes was for president and which was for vice president, both Jefferson and Aaron Burr received the same number of votes. Burr refused to concede and the election went to the House of Representatives, where it took 36 ballots before Jefferson eventually won.
2. To preside over the U.S. Senate
3. a. 8
   b. 4: Calvin Coolidge, Theodore Roosevelt, Harry Truman, Lyndon Johnson
   c. Gerald Ford
   d. 5: John Adams, Thomas Jefferson, Martin Van Buren, Richard Nixon, George Bush

The Campaign page 23
1. Much of it comes from private donations by wealthy people. Some of it is donated through dinner and telephone requests. Some is raised through small individual donations. Special-interest groups donate money to candidates' campaigns. The federal government also makes some funds available to candidates.

2. There was a concern that, without restrictions, certain individuals and special-interest groups would hold hostage a candidate's views in exchange for a lot of money.
3. Limits were placed on the amount of money any single individual can give to a candidate.
   The government has now made money available to candidates of the major parties.

Press Coverage of the Campaign   page 25
1. Answers will vary.
2. Answers will vary.
3. Answers will vary.

Opinion Polls   page 26
Answers will vary.

Election Day   page 28
1. Answers will vary but should include comments about the primary rights afforded Americans in almost all aspects of life.
2. Answers will vary, but students will probably agree that such pronouncements do discourage West Coast voters from even going to the polls.
3. 538 electoral votes are available. It takes 269 +1 = 270 to win a simple majority.
4. The electors from the various states meet in their state capitals on the Monday after the second Wednesday in December following the November elections.

George Washington   page 30
1. North Carolina and Rhode Island had not yet ratified the Constitution. New York was unable to decide in time to send delegates.
2. They favored a strong central government that could control the states rather than the states controlling it.
3. John Adams
4. Each elector was allowed to cast two votes. In both elections Washington received one of those two votes from every elector.
5. The Federalists favored a strong central government. The Republicans favored a diffusion of power from the federal government level down to the states.

John Adams   page 32
1. a. Adams   d. Jefferson
   b. Adams   e. Adams
   c. Jefferson   f. Jefferson
2. Because each elector got two votes, Hamilton wanted the southern electors to vote for Thomas Pinkney and anyone else except Adams, and by trusting that the New England Federalists would vote for Adams and Pinkney, Hamilton hoped to make Pinkney the president.
3. New Englanders heard of the plan and thus reduced Pinkney's total, dragging below not only Adams, but also Jefferson who became Adams' vice president.
4. Growing hostilities with France caused Adams to send a three-man delegation to try to resolve the differences. But Prime Minister Tallyrand refused to see them directly and sent three unknowns to the American delegation, demanding a payment of $250,000 before he would consider normalizing relations. Americans regarded this as blackmail and Adams substituted the French names with the letters X, Y, and Z. For two years the two countries were on the brink of war.

Thomas Jefferson   page 34
1. The House of Representatives voted 36 times before finally electing Jefferson. Alexander Hamilton played a key role in bringing Federalist support to Jefferson, as he considered him the lesser of two evils. The entire absurdity of the process revealed the need for reform in the manner of electing the president.
2. Under the Twelfth Amendment, candidates from each party were nominated for president. Then each had a running mate chosen to run as vice president. It now became a matter of voting for a pair of candidates rather than a single person being the president and the runner-up becoming the vice president.
3. For $15 million (approximately 3¢/acre), the United States bought from France the Louisiana Territory, a vast region between the Rockies and the Mississippi. Jefferson had only authorized his buyer to purchase New Orleans (to gain access to the Mississippi) and west Florida. But Napoleon needed the cash to wage war against Britain, so he offered the entire land parcel. Jefferson jumped at the deal even though its constitutionality was in question. The Senate eventually ratified the treaty, and the size of the young country was doubled.

James Madison   page 36
1. The embargo posed hardship for those who were involved in manufacturing. Most of the industrial might of the country was located in the Northeast, which was hurt the most.
2. Answers will vary.
3. Madison defended the war as being necessary to establish America's neutral rights to stop the practice of impressment. Clinton sought to win votes on both sides and really never took much of a position other than to criticize Madison.
4. Madison 128, Clinton 89; Madison won 11 states, Clinton won 7, mostly in New England. Madison's support came from the South and West.
5. The Treaty of Ghent, negotiated in December of 1814, ended the war with both sides keeping the land held prior to the war. Communication being a problem, the Battle of New Orleans was fought after the peace treaty was signed.

James Monroe   page 38
1. The Federalists had claimed that the war had no meaning and should not have been fought. Republicans felt it necessary to defend America's right to neutrality. The Federalist position on the war brought the virtual end to a dying party.
2. Governor William Plumer of New Hampshire cast the single vote for John Quincy Adams. Some say he did this to preserve Washington's record as the only president unanimously chosen by the electoral college, but he claimed to have voted honestly against Monroe.
3. The law maintained the balance between slave and free states by admitting Maine as a free state and Missouri as a slave state. It further established that all future states north of the line 36°30′ would be free states, and all states south of the line would be slave states. Monroe was against the law, but he signed it anyway.

4. It warned the rest of the world to stay out of the Americas. Any future colonization by foreign powers would not be tolerated.

John Quincy Adams   page 40
1. John Quincy Adams—New England
   Andrew Jackson—Tennessee and other states in the West
   Henry Clay—Kentucky and other states in the West
   William H. Crawford—states in the South
2. John Quincy Adams   115,696   84
   Andrew Jackson   162,933   99
   Henry Clay   47,136   37
   William H. Crawford   46,979   41
3. Because no candidate received a majority of electors, the election was to be decided in the House of Representatives. Article II, section 1. But the Twelfth Amendment reduced the list to the top three from the electoral college to be on the list that goes to the House of Representatives.
4. Since each state got only one vote in the House of Representatives, Henry Clay (who had received the fourth highest total in the electoral vote) supported Adams and Adams was thus able to gain enough states to win the election in the House.
5. He was furious and almost immediately began campaigning for the next election.

Andrew Jackson   page 42
1. The South had been disturbed by Jackson's vote for the tariff while he was in the Senate. But having Calhoun as a running mate helped him win the South (as Calhoun was from South Carolina).
2. Jackson supporters seethed at the way the election of 1824 had been handled. They became known as the Jacksonian Democrats. Adams' supporters called themselves National Republicans. At the time the main difference was the tariff, which was favored by New England manufacturers and opposed by Southern farmers.
3. Jackson firmly believed "to the victor belong the spoils," so he did appoint some of his friends to jobs in government. But in reality, he replaced only about 15 percent of the government workers during his administration.
4. Jackson was displeased with most of the members of his cabinet, so he began to seek advice from friends and relatives. He abandoned regular cabinet meetings and met privately with this group of advisors he trusted in what came to be known as the Kitchen Cabinet

Martin Van Buren   page 44
1. He said that Congress did indeed have the right to abolish slavery in the nation's capital. But he quickly went on to say that he was opposed to any interference with slavery in the South.
2. Martin Van Buren   170
   William Henry Harrison   73
   Hugh Lawson White   26
   Daniel Webster   14
   Willie P. Mangum   11
                               294
3. Virginia electors supported Van Buren but refused to support Richard Johnson. Without the votes from Virginia, Johnson lacked a majority of electoral votes; hence the election was decided by the U.S. Senate. This is the only time this has ever happened.
4. There were 294 electors. A majority would be 148. Virginia had 23 electoral votes. Thus 170 - 23 = 147. Johnson needed only one more vote to avoid having the election decided in the U.S. Senate. He did win the election in the Senate anyway.

William Henry Harrison   page 46
1. While Harrison actually grew up on the grand Berkeley estate in Virginia and lived in a stately 22-room manor in North Bend, Ohio, he did not mind (nor did the Whigs) the log-cabin image, because it made him look more like a candidate of the people who were distancing themselves from Martin Van Buren.
2. Harrison had become a war hero with his victory over the Shawnee Indians at the Battle of Tippecanoe. The phrase became catchy with the addition of "Tyler, too." John Tyler was his vice-presidential running mate.
3. was for limited exercise of federal authority
   was for deposit of federal funds in independent banks
   was opposed to federally funded internal improvements
   was opposed to a planned treasury surplus, interference with slavery, and a protective tariff
4. The economic depression that accompanied the panic of 1837, which occurred just two months after Van Buren's inauguration. The depression actually lasted until 1843. The Whigs did not say how they would correct the situation, just that they would restore prosperity.

John Tyler   pages 47 and 48
1. The Whig Party chose Tyler because they wanted to gain support in the South and felt that Tyler could help do this.
2. Some doubted that he had any rights and power beyond that of serving as acting president. Tyler denied this and from the beginning regarded himself as the president. He ran the office with this philosophy.
3. Tyler refused to endorse the Whig Party's attempt to restore a national bank. Hence the Whig cabinet members from Harrison's administration resigned.
4. His refusal to support Whig efforts to restore a national bank made him an outcast with the Whig Party.
5. Tyler and Southern states thought that Texas had the potential to become several states. They wanted to give the South greater power in Congress.

James Polk   page 50
1. D, W, W, D, D, W, D, W
2. Clay hurt his chances in the South by opposing the annexation of Texas. In the North he was undercut by a third-party candidate, James Buchanan, who took valuable votes from Clay.
3. A dark-horse candidate is one who is the underdog, often chosen as a compromise candidate when none of the favorites can emerge as the winner. Such was the case of Polk.

Zachary Taylor   page 52

1. It was a bill before Congress to ban slavery from any territory that was acquired as a result of the Mexican War. Taylor owned more than 100 slaves, so he won a lot of Southern support without offering any comment. Cass was very much against it and preferred what he called "squatter sovereignty," i.e., allowing the people to decide for themselves.
2. Van Buren gained enough votes from antislavery Democrats to cause Cass to lose states he felt he would win. Van Buren did not actually win any states, but he got enough votes from the Democrats to allow the Whig candidate to win a number of Democratic states.
3. Taylor was a war hero in the Mexican War. Following the war, "Old Rough and Ready" became a popular national hero, and he easily won the Whig nomination.

Millard Fillmore   page 54

1. Fillmore indicated to Taylor that he would vote in favor of the Compromise of 1850 because he believed in it (if there was a tie in the Senate, Fillmore would get to cast the deciding vote) even though Taylor was much opposed to it.
2. 1. California was admitted as a free state.
   2. Borders of Texas were defined and Texas received $40 million to pay off war debt.
   3. Territory of Utah was established.
   4. Fugitive Slave Law required the federal government to take an active part in returning all fugitive slaves to their owners.
   5. Slave trade was abolished in Washington, D.C.
3. He sent Perry with four warships to Japan to obtain pledges from Japan to rescue shipwrecked Americans and to open at least one port to U.S. trade. Actually, two ports were opened and active trade with Japan began.

Franklin Pierce   page 56

1. Polk was the Democratic dark-horse candidate in the election of 1844 and was successful in winning the presidency. The Democrats were hoping that their second dark-horse candidate, Franklin Pierce, would also win in 1852.
2. Pierce was not opposed to the spread of slavery because he said the U.S. Constitution protected property, and slaves were property. He had a real hatred for abolitionists.
3. The Whig Party was somewhat divided over the issue of slavery, while the Democratic Party fully supported the Compromise of 1850. In the end the voters overwhelmingly voted for the dark-horse, Franklin Pierce.

James Buchanan   pages 57 and 58

1. They were much against it! Southern Democrats warned that a Republican victory would lead to Civil War.
2. The issue of slavery was more serious than Buchanan imagined.
   slavery—He was against slavery but recognized it as a necessary evil.
   Fugitive Slave Act—He supported the Fugitive Slave Act
   Dred Scott Decision—He welcomed the decision because it proclaimed that blacks were not citizens.
3. He was engaged to Anne Coleman, the daughter of a Pennsylvania millionaire. The two quarreled and she returned to Philadelphia and died quite suddenly—possibly from suicide. Buchanan was heartbroken and he never pursued anyone else.

Abraham Lincoln   page 60

1. secession from the Union—called such acts treason
   slavery in the territories—end to slavery in the territories
   slavery in the South—upheld slavery in the South
   Dred Scott Decision—denounced the decision
2. He felt that slavery would need to be continued in the South if there was to be any hope of saving the Union.
3. The victory of Sherman at Atlanta marked the turning of the tide in favor of the North. The Democrats, who had called for an immediate armistice, now were shackled in a futile attempt to salvage votes—which they did not. Lincoln won easily.

Andrew Johnson   page 62

1. Johnson had been a Southern Democrat who remained loyal to the Union. Thus Lincoln hoped to win votes in the border states that had remained loyal to the Union.
2. Johnson had vetoed the Tenure of Office Act, which forbade the president to remove certain public officials without the consent of the Senate. Johnson had dismissed Secretary of War Stanton, so the House of Representatives voted to impeach him 126-47.
3. To remove a president from office requires a 2/3 majority in the U.S. Senate.
4. Of the 11 articles brought against him, the Senate voted 35-19 on the eleventh article, just one vote shy of the necessary 2/3 needed. Ten days later he was acquitted by the same margin of two other articles. The remaining eight articles were never brought before the Senate.

Ulysses S. Grant   pages 63 and 64

1. After four years of Civil War and three years of wrangling over Reconstruction, the nation craved the peace promised them by Grant.
2. He was a hero.
3. He chose many of his friends as cabinet members and other high-ranking officials. They were not qualified and some were dishonest. Grant himself had no political background. He was a war hero, and war heroes seldom have made good presidents.

Rutherford B. Hayes   page 66

1. The Democrats assumed that Colorado would become a Democratic state. It did not, and its three electoral votes cost the Democrats the election by a vote of 185 for Hayes to 184 for Tilden.
2. Congress appointed a 15-man electoral commission. It was composed of five congressmen, five senators, and five Supreme Court justices. All voted strictly by party and the commission voted 8-7 to give all three states in dispute to Hayes. Hayes was as surprised as anyone to find out that he had won.

3. He appointed many Democrats to positions of power, and he ended all military occupation in the Southern states.

James A. Garfield   page 68

1. Garfield won the highly populated states in the East—states that had the most electoral votes.
2. Garfield was assassinated by Charles Guiteau, a disappointed office seeker who had supported Garfield's election. Garfield died of blood poisoning that occurred because those who tended to Garfield used bare fingers and unsterilized instruments. Guiteau was hanged for his deed.

Chester A. Arthur   page 70

1. When Garfield won the nomination (which was a surprise), the Republicans needed a member of the New York Stalwarts to add strength to the party ticket. Garfield's first choice was Levi Morton, but he declined. Garfield then asked Arthur, who was honored by the nomination.
2. Arthur realized that as president, he should put his support of the spoils system behind him and run the office with integrity. This he tried to do.
3. Answers will vary, but honesty, virtue, integrity, and willingness to work very hard should be among the choices.

Grover Cleveland   page 72

1. Blaine was implicated in charges that he had earlier profited from his association with railroad interests while he was a member of Congress.
2. During Cleveland's earlier years, he had an affair with an alcoholic young widow from New Jersey. She had a child and named Cleveland as the father. He didn't deny this and people loved him for his honesty.
3. A remark made by Reverend Samuel Burchard, a Presbyterian minister at a meeting of ministers and Blaine, in which he proclaimed that the Republicans would vote for Blaine because they didn't want to be associated with "Rum, Romanism, and Rebellion." This remark went unchallenged by Blaine, which caused many Catholics to vote for Cleveland as their way of protesting Blaine.

Benjamin Harrison   page 74

1. 5,540,329 Cleveland
   5,439,853 Harrison
   100,476 more votes for Cleveland
2. The reform-minded Cleveland made many enemies in the famous Tammany Hall political machine that controlled much of New York. Many of the more influential members campaigned vigorously for Harrison and helped to carry New York and thus deny Cleveland the votes he needed to win.
3. Answers will vary, but a firm handshake is considered synonymous with good manners. A weak handshake is considered by many to be a cold and impersonal way to greet people. Most people who aspire to success have a very firm handshake.

Grover Cleveland   page 76

1. James B. Weaver of the Populist Party won the states of Colorado, Idaho, Kansas, and Nevada. One of the big reasons he won these states was his support for the free coinage of silver, which all western states supported.
2. Answers will vary, but his honesty and integrity in government stand out among his most important virtues . . . and these virtues are timeless.
3. Answers will vary but probably will involve discussion about his winning the popular vote over Benjamin Harrison.

William McKinley   page 78

1. Answers will vary, but today's world of politics requires vigorous, aggressive campaigning to be competitive in the elections.
2. Americans had four prosperous years during the first administration of William McKinley. The full dinner pail made reference to plenty to eat for most Americans during these prosperous times.
3. Spain relinquished its claims to Cuba and ceded Puerto Rico, Guam, and for $20 million the Philippine Islands to the United States.

Theodore Roosevelt   page 80

1. Answers will vary, but the press plays a large role in today's world of portraying the image of the nation's president. Thus, it's important for him to have a positive image.
2. Roosevelt won the popular vote by over 2 million votes. His winning percentage was 56% to 38%. His victory was pretty much nationwide except for the Democratic South.
3. Answers will vary, but he kept his nation out of war, he mediated a war between Japan and Russia, he supported a revolution in Panama to further his plans to build a canal there, and he designated land for national parks. He was one of America's most assertive presidents. In short, he got things done.

William Howard Taft   page 82

1. Bryan wanted to nationalize the railroads. The Republicans and the American public viewed this as socialism, something they did not want.
2. It was a term used to encourage Americans investing in foreign countries to help ensure their success. With American dollars at stake, Taft said we had the right to put down rebellions and bring in military troops to protect American investments. He claimed that it was nothing more than an extension of the Monroe Doctrine.
3. When Roosevelt returned from a lengthy African safari, he found some disappointments in his hand-picked successor. He regarded Taft's administration as too conservative and claimed that Taft was not doing enough with antitrust legislation. The two became real political enemies at the 1912 Republican Convention, and the rift continued until 1918, when the two settled their differences in a Chicago restaurant.

Woodrow Wilson   page 84

1. Answers will vary, but the obvious reason Wilson won was because the Democrats were divided between the incumbent William Howard Taft and former President Theodore Roosevelt.
2. Answers will vary, but Wilson did win most of the populous states that had large numbers of electors plus he actually won the popular vote by 3%.

© Instructional Fair • TS Denison   123   IF87033 Electing Our President: Campaigns and Elections

Warren G. Harding   **page 86**
1. Cox wholeheartedly supported America's joining the League as a way of ensuring world peace. Harding was very much against America's participation in the League on Wilson's terms and contributed much to its eventual failure.
2. Secretary of the Interior Albert Fall; Thomas Miller, a property owner convicted of accepting bribes; Jess Smith, also involved in Teapot Dome Affair; Charles Forbes, director of the Veteran Bureau; Charles Cramer, an aid to Forbes
3. Answers will vary.

Calvin Coolidge   **page 88**
1. The term did not imply "hip" or "groovy" or "with it" as it does today. The term referred to calm, serene, and impenetrable. Since Coolidge was all of the above, he had no trouble riding the coattails of this philosophy to victory.
2. Answers will vary, but today's world calls for a president who is committed to every issue for every hour of every day.

Herbert Hoover   **page 90**
1. It implied the prosperity the country was currently experiencing should continue. There was also the implication that no one would be hungry.
2. 1. Probably Smith being a Catholic hurt his chances for election.
   2. He was also outspoken against Prohibition.
   3. Americans were quite content with the apparently strong economy under the Republican Coolidge administration. Why would they want to change?
3. 1. Surplus of agricultural products depressed farm prices
   2. Lack of credit restraints; stocks could be purchased for as little as a 25-percent margin.
   3. High tariffs discouraged world trade.
   4. Acceleration of corporate profits at the expense of higher wages for workers lowered purchasing power.

Franklin Delano Roosevelt   **pages 92–94**
1. Hoover often faced hostile crowds and he did not handle it well. His speeches sounded desperate and he was often unsteady in his delivery. Roosevelt promised farmers he would stabilize prices. He promised public works projects for the jobless. He promised increased benefits to failing businesses. His plan was called the New Deal.
2. Roosevelt won by a landslide. 57% of the popular vote to 40% for Hoover. He won the electoral election 472 to 59.
3. He claimed that the waste and inefficiency of the president's policies were slowing the recovery process. He claimed he could speed up the process of recovery if elected, but he really did not say how he planned to do it.
4. Maine and Vermont
5. Answers will vary.
6. Wilkie won the farm vote, and he won the vote of the villages, the towns, and the small cities. But Roosevelt won all the big cities and major metropolitan areas, which explains how he handily won the election.
7. Roosevelt's fourth victory was his closest. He still won the popular vote 53% to 46% for Dewey and the electoral vote 432 to 99. But it was not considered a landslide.

Harry S Truman   **page 96**
1. They felt he had "inherited" the presidency as a result of the death of FDR and that he could not win on his own.
2. Campaign term used to indicate making campaign stops at remote and not-so-populous places. Truman traveled many miles on trains and appealed to the people with his candor and honesty.
3. Truman 49% of popular vote, Dewey 45%, Thurmond 2%, Wallace 2% In electoral vote Truman won 303 to Dewey's 189 to Thurmond's 39. Sophisticated computers and other technology available today can predict with accuracy how elections will turn out.

Dwight D. Eisenhower   **page 98**
1. Eisenhower came across as a friendly, folksy, common, ordinary smiling candidate, while Stevenson portrayed an image of a cold, formal, "egghead." The public overwhelmingly chose Ike.
2. The Democratic campaign was very low on funds, and the Republicans landed on the hole-in-Stevenson's shoe with a slogan of "Don't Let This Happen to You!" Implied the Democrats would bring poverty to America.
3. He launched a reasonably vigorous campaign to show Americans that he had fully recovered from his heart attack and was once again healthy.
4. Eisenhower loved to play golf, even though he was not very good. The implications of the slogan were:
   1. He played too much golf, thus not spending enough time at his job.
   2. Since Hogan was the premier golfer of the day, the people should elect him if they wanted a golfer to be their president.

John F. Kennedy   **page 100**
1. During the debates Kennedy appeared tan, trim, and composed. Nixon, on the other hand, had lost weight during an illness and came across to the American public as haggard, pale, and menacing.
2. Kennedy 34,227,096   49.7%
   Nixon 34,108,546   49.5%
   Kennedy won by 118,000 votes, less than .4 of one percent!
3. Dr. Martin Luther King, Jr., had been arrested in a civil rights march in Atlanta. Kennedy sent a personal apology to Mrs. King, and his brother Robert was able to get King released from jail. King's father deeply appreciated Kennedy's courage and influenced blacks to vote for him.

Lyndon B. Johnson   **page 102**
1. Goldwater opposed civil rights and stressed the need to restore freedom in American life. He felt that people should have the right to associate with minorities if they so chose or have the right not to associate with minorities if that was their choice.

2. Because Goldwater was such a right-wing conservative, the Democrats were warning the American public against associating themselves with such radical thinking.
3. Johnson 43,126, 506, 61% 486 electors 90.7%
   Goldwater 27,176,799, 39% 52 electors 9.3%

Richard M. Nixon   **page 104**
1. Over 5,000 demonstrators against the war in Southeast Asia clashed with Chicago police during the 1968 Democratic convention. The unpopularity of the war also caused many Americans to blame the Johnson administration. Nixon claimed to have a "secret plan" to end the war. He did not have such a plan, but he won the election anyway.
2. McGovern's promise to give every American $1,000, to withdraw immediately from Vietnam, plus his lack of support for Senator Eagleton as his running mate made him a suspicious candidate among most Americans, and Nixon won by a landslide.

Gerald R. Ford   **page 106**
1. Answers will vary.
2. Because there was no plan under the original Constitution to provide steps for selecting a new vice president when the vice president became president, the Twenty-fifth Amendment was proposed and ratified. It also provided for a smooth transition for times when the vice president might need to take over for the president on a temporary basis. Ford chose Nelson A. Rockefeller of New York as his vice president.
3. Johnson disagreed with Ford on a number of issues, and he even doubted his intelligence at times (which he implied by this statement).
   Reagan criticized Ford for downplaying of the military during his administration.

Jimmy Carter   **page 108**
1. national health insurance—Democrats were in favor of it; Republicans opposed it.
   abortion—Democrats favored the right of choice; Republicans wanted a constitutional amendment against it.
   expenditures on national defense—Democrats favored cuts in defense spending; Republicans wanted increased spending for defense.
   control of the Panama Canal—Democrats favored a treaty that guarded U.S. interests; Republicans wanted to retain the canal.
   busing students to achieve racial equality in school—Democrats wanted it only as a last resort; Republicans favored an amendment to ban busing altogether.
2. Deep South—Jimmy Carter
   Industrial North—Jimmy Carter
   West—Ford
   Carter won 50% of the popular vote to 48% for Ford. In the electoral vote, Carter won 297 to 240.

Ronald Reagan   **page 110**
1. He had promised inflation of no more than 4%, while it turned out to be more than 10%.
   He pledged to cut defense spending, and he actually increased it.
   He allowed the giant oil companies to make windfall profits.
   The hostage crisis continued in Iran.
2. Deficit Spending—Democrats usually supported it, and Republicans favored a balanced budget. Reagan's first term led the nation into record debt, while Mondale sought a balanced budget.
   Foreign trade—Democrats usually supported freer trade and reduced tariffs while Republicans favored protective tariffs to ensure higher prices at home. Reagan, on the other hand, opposed protectionist measures and hoped to trade more abroad. Mondale called for import quotes.

George Bush   **page 112**
1. George Bush—execution of drug traffickers; supported Star Wars missile system; vowed to never raise taxes; voluntary prayer in school; constitutional amendment to ban abortion
   Micheal Dukakis—national health insurance plan; opposed Star Wars defense expansion; step up tax collections against those who cheated; employee-financed health insurance; federal tuition loans; attacked capital gains tax cut
2. Bush; The vote was split between Bush and Dukakis; Dukakis; 47,946,422, 54%; 41,016,429, 46%; 426; 111

Bill Clinton   **page 114**
1. Clinton   44,908,233   43%
   Bush   39,102,282   37%
   Perot   19,741,048   19%
   Electoral votes—Clinton 370; Bush 168
2. In 1996 Clinton received 45,628,667 49% to Dole's 37,869,435 41% to Perot's 7,874,423 8%.
   Clinton won the electoral vote 379 to Dole's 159—winning all the states he had won in 1992 plus Florida.

Election Trivia I   **page 115**
1. c	4. b	7. b	10. c
2. a	5. b	8. a	11. c
3. c	6. b	9. b	12. a

Election Trivia II   **page 117**
1. b	4. c	7. b	10. a
2. a	5. a	8. b	11. a
3. a	6. b	9. c	12. b

Election Trivia III   **page 119**
1. a	4. c	7. c	10. c
2. b	5. b	8. a	11. b
3. a	6. b	9. b	12. a